D1045308

Geoffrey Elborn

THE DEDALUS BOOK OF VODKA

Dedalus

Published in the UK by Dedalus Limited,
24-26, St Judith's Lane, Sawtry, Cambs, PE28 5XE
email: info@dedalusbooks.com
www.dedalusbooks.com

ISBN printed book 978 1 907650 04 8
ISBN ebook book 978 1 909232 62 4

Dedalus is distributed in the USA & Canada by SCB Distributors,
15608 South New Century Drive, Gardena, CA 90248
email: info@scbdistributors.com web: www.scbdistributors.com

Dedalus is distributed in Australia by Peribo Pty Ltd.
58, Beaumont Road, Mount Kuring-gai, N.S.W. 2080
email: info@peribo.com.au

First published by Dedalus in 2013

Printed in Finland by Bookwell
Typeset by Marie Lane

A C.I.P. listing for this book is available on request.

The Author

Geoffrey Elborn was born in Edinburgh where he worked as a librarian before studying English and Music in York.

After publishing a volume of poetry, he was asked by Sacheverell Sitwell to write a life of his sister Edith. He then went on to write several more biographies. He has written for many journals and magazines including *The Glasgow Herald*, *The Guardian*, *The Times*, *The Tablet*, *The Scotsman*, *Tempo* and *The Proms Seasons Concert Programmes*. He has contributed to several books including *The Oxford Dictionary of National Biography.*

To

Mark Watson

and the discarnate spirits of

Ted and I.G.P

Contents

Introduction

[Miss Matfield]… had never tasted vodka before, never remembered ever having seen it before, but of course it was richly associated with her memories of romantic fiction of various kinds, and was tremendously thrilling… as the liquor slipped over her palate… it was if an incendiary bomb had burst in her throat and sent white fire racing down every channel of her body. She gasped, laughed, coughed, all at once.

Angel Pavement, J. B. Priestley, 1930

There cannot be not enough snacks,
There can only be not enough vodka.
There can be no silly jokes,
There can only be not enough vodka.
There can be no ugly women,
There can only be not enough vodka.
There cannot be too much vodka,
There can only be not enough vodka.

Russian saying

Vodka is the best-selling spirit in the world. The popularity of the "green wine", five hundred years old in Russia and Poland, is now shared in America and Europe where it emerged as the drink of the young midway through the 20th century. The sheer versatility of vodka, regardless of where and when it was drunk, has ensured its survival, but it was virtually unknown in Britain until the 1960s.

Tchaikovsky knew all about vodka, for he drank it nearly every day and had set a folk song to music, which began, "Don't go, my son, to the tsar's tavern… Don't drink, my son, any green wine." When he was in London to conduct his Fourth Symphony for its British premiere on 2 June 1893, the composer's English was inadequate to convey during a rehearsal exactly how he wanted the orchestra to play in the last, fast movement. "Failing to get the reckless Russian spirit he wanted, [he] eventually obtained it by exclaiming, 'Vodka – more vodka!!'" It was fortunate that the orchestra understood what he meant given that vodka's success across the British Isles lay far into the future.

The absence of vodka in Britain was amusingly commented on by the great Russian writer Ivan Turgenev, whose novel of 1859, *A House of Gentlefolk*, includes a character who has visited England before returning to his own country as a complete "Anglomaniac". He changes his appearance and household arrangements with the result that, "his passion for roast beef and port wine – everything about him – breathed, so to speak, of Great Britain… breakfast began to be served in a different way; foreign wines replaced vodka and syrups…"

The first recorded mention in the British press of domestic consumption came in a footnote to an account of the Brewers Annual Exhibition in the Agricultural Hall of Islington, London on 16 October 1905. Despite the confident assertion that, " a point which is perhaps worth a passing mention for those who follow the fashions in such things is that vodka is now coming into vogue", the writer was mistaken.

It would be another fifty years before vodka became fashionable, and Miss Matfield only experienced her taste of the "white fire" in J.B. Priestley's 1930 novel, *Angel Pavement*, because it was given to her on board a Baltic ship that was tied up in a London dock.

Whether enjoyed at home, in the comfort of a luxury bar or a scruffy pub, vodka will contribute to a good, and fairly harmless, night of pleasure. If no other alcohol is mixed with it, the purity of the spirit lessens the chance of a hangover the following day.

The fruit-flavoured vodkas now widely consumed in Europe and

America began life in Russia and Poland, where the best of its kind was made with fresh fruit. In 19th-century Moscow, the fruit destined for the vodka distilleries arrived by the cartload, drawn by horses struggling through filthy, narrow and boggy streets. Brightly alluring in a beautifully-shaped bottle, a Smirnov fruit-based speciality such as rowanberry vodka might be destined for the tsar's table or a high-class restaurant. It would then be devoured along with *zakuski*, the carefully prepared traditional snacks, which formed a delicious prelude to a main meal. Foreigners' lack of familiarity with *zakuski* in the 19th century was noted with amusement when some English visitors were invited to a reception in one of Moscow's imperial palaces. They devoured so many of the small snacks intended to be eaten with the vodka that the waiters had to replenish the supply on several occasions. The visitors were embarrassed to discover that a banquet awaited them in the next room.

Such culinary refinements would not be particularly appreciated by the hardened vodka drinkers of Moscow. Many were homeless beggars who drank the spirit neat and would drink it whenever and wherever they could find it. The most squalid dosshouses typically catered for the kopek-less vodka drinker. The foul Khitrov market, located in present-day Gorky Park, was constantly packed with thieves and down-and-outs. If they could part with a few coins for something hot, one notorious canteen supplied a tasty soup made from scraps of meat and bones that were salvaged from restaurants' pig bins. Chopped and mashed to a pulp with added bay leaves and generous spoonfuls of pepper, it was a gourmet feast for the half-frozen alcoholics who suffered through the winter wandering the icy Moscow streets.

But there was no need to feel desperate if you had spent nearly all of your money on the soup and thought for a dreadful moment that the rest of the evening would have to be endured without vodka. Although it could not match the quality of the spirit on offer in the imperial palaces, vodka was in plentiful and cheap supply in the dosshouses situated in illegal premises across the city.

Like the tasty soup, the vodka was the product of leftovers. In many taverns, a man was employed to open the bottled vodka with the aid of a corkscrew. Usually an old drunk, he sat with a mug, which he used to accumulate dribbles of vodka that had been left behind in cups and bottles. Once he had collected a measure of about half a bottle, approximately 300ml, it was bought by anyone who could not afford an entire bottle, which was the only container in which vodka could be legally sold.

The same filthy vodka waste was also supplied to dosshouse landlords for a small payment, guaranteeing euphoric nights on floorboards or filthy mattresses for the residents. Although food was supposed to be available in the dosshouses, a female inmate's remark at the time – "there wasn't nothing to eat but I drank three glasses of vodka!" – probably typified the general situation.

For the homeless who loved vodka in the 19th century in Russia, only the fiery spirit mattered in their otherwise barren lives. Indeed, from the 15th century onwards, vodka had mattered to all Russians from Peter the Great and his fellow tsars to the merchant and peasant classes. It has always had more of an impact in Russia than other neighbouring countries such as Poland, which also claim to be its rightful birthplace.

As the American actor and political commentator Will Rogers wrote in 1927:

> Nobody in the world knows what vodka is made out of, and the reason I tell you that is that the story of vodka is the story of Russia. Nobody knows what Russia is made of, or what it is liable to cause its inhabitants to do next.

This book aims to tell that story of Russia and its relationship with vodka and the experiences of all the people who have loved it, those who have hated it as well as those who have simply enjoyed vodka wherever the spirit has been served – from palaces and the lowliest taverns to Hollywood bars and London nightclubs. As will become apparent, no spirit has influenced affairs of state to the extent achieved by the green wine.

Part 1

The Drink of the Slavs

A Russian Kabak in the 19th century

Russian Imperial Vodka late 19th century

Part1

I

The Russian Story

> *Oxford English Dictionary* definition of vodka:
>
> Forms: Also vodki, vodky, wodky; y. votku, votky
>
> Etymology: Russian vodka (genitive singular vodki), pronounced 'votka'.
>
> An ardent spirit used orig. esp. in Russia, chiefly distilled from rye, but also from barley, potatoes, or other material.

The "other material" could also be: whey, molasses, soya beans, grapes, rice, sugar beets, the results of oil refining or wood-pulp processing. Use of the latter ingredient almost verifies the claims of a Soviet comic hero that vodka can be made from a stool.

The *Oxford English Dictionary* definition is all very well, but it does not mention that vodka means "dear little water", a diminutive of the word "voda", or "water" in Russian. To be fair, it may not be Russian in origin as Poland called the same liquid "wodka".

A Mr Kohl, a German visitor to St. Petersburg in the 1840s, was fascinated by vodka, and without realising it, not only described the whole problem of the spirit itself as consumed by Russians but also the confusion over what it was to be called:

> Among all the Slavonic nations, and especially the Russians, brandy is becoming so mighty a divinity, that in the same sense as we say, "Money rules the world", we might say of it, "Brandy rules the Russians". The usual *douceur* in Russia is a *rumka wodki* (a glass of brandy); the ordinary recompense, the ordinary medium of bribery with the common man, is not money, but brandy. It is worthy of remark that the people of the lower class are not so thankful for the former as the latter: neither Sunday nor any remarkable day, neither Easter nor Christmas, passes without it. With brandy the soldier is primed for the battle; with brandy the listless labourer is incited to exertion. The avidity of the Russians for this fiery poison is astonishing. Brandy is a liquor introduced by foreigners among the Russians, though they have now a name of their own invention for it; they call it *wodica* … [which] is become the principal and almost exclusive soother of the cares of the common Russians. *Wodka! wodka! wodka! rumka wodki*, ought to occur at least ten times on every page of a Russian dictionary which should pretend to convey a proper idea of the frequent use of a word and its importance. Thousands of persons in Russia become rich through the immense consumption of brandy and millions poor.

Kohl's confusion of the actual name, calling it *brandy*, then *vodica* and later *wodka*, was not the ignorance of a foreigner. For if he had looked the word up in a Russian dictionary, he would not have found it, even though it was used in speech to describe a particular kind of flavoured vodka. "Vodka" was not a fixture of Russian dictionaries until the 1860s. This proved to be a headache for translators of foreigners' accounts of visits to Russia, who found there no word they could use, and many simply used "whisky" or "brandy" to mean "a spirit", with confusing results.

The word "vodka" probably first appeared in English in 1780

when a book on Russia written by a German writer was published in London. It appeared as part of a footnote to explain the word *kabak*:

> *Kabak* in the Russian language signifies a public house for the common people to drink *vodka* (a sort of brandy) in.

It was first mentioned in an original English language text by two Scotsmen who perhaps used it in order to avoid confusion between their own native drink and Russia's. A Captain Cochrane, who drank vodka while travelling through Russia in 1820, described it as "vodka (whisky)". The earliest descriptive use of the word in English was by Robert Lyall in 1823. He noticed a crown-bonded warehouse in Moscow, which was so large that it took up two immense squares, and its thick walls were covered by a vaulted roof. It contained thousands of barrels of vodka transported to it by distillers from across the country. Their contents were then sold to the taverns and people living in the Moscow area. In anticipation of the arrival of Napoleon's marauding troops, orders were given in 1812 to empty the warehouse. Rivers of vodka ran down the street in rivers before being drunk by a mob of the city's poorest who licked the pavement for the last drop. According to Lyall, the spirit was:

> Precious *votki,* the nectar of the Russian peasants, which is measured in strength by the hydrometer, and sold according to law. Good *votki* by no means deserves the reproach thrown upon it by some travellers. As sold in the *kabaks* and in the shops, it is generally diluted and adulterated, and certainly is a fiery, slowly operating poison. It resembles Scotch whisky. It is a kind of proof spirit, according to pharmaceutical phraseology. It is called brandy by the mistakes of travellers, and sometimes Russian brandy…

Lyall examined previous travel writers' musings on Russia and frequently came across the misuse of "Russian brandy" in all senses of the word. The misnaming of the spirit by foreign travellers would continue through the remainder of the 19th century, but with exceptions such as Lyall, nearly all agreed that it was "vile".

By 1865 vodka appeared in Murray's *Handbook for Travellers in Russia, Poland and Finland* and was referred to as "corn brandy". The book also included useful phrases such as "drink money", *Na vodka*; "I will give you drink money", *Dam Na vodku*; "I will not give you drink money", *Ne dam na vodku.*

The drink was otherwise to be avoided in unmentionable taverns:

> Events of a... festive character are celebrated at establishments where the bottle and the glass replace the more steady teapot, especially since the price of vodka has been made very low. Those establishments need not be inspected; their effect will be painfully seen in the tottering *moujik* [peasant] and the oblivious woman jolting home in a *drojky* [a low, four-wheeled open carriage] or waiting to be picked up from the gutter.

In Russia itself, a lengthy catalogue of other written names were used to refer to the spirit. They described what was in essence *vodka* but were in fact different drinks, identified often by the number of times they were refined, the amount of water added, the flavouring used and the strength. The longer the process, the more costly the result, as each refining process reduced the volume of liquid.

Vodka drunk in taverns was the first result of distillation and called *raka.* The next upgrade was "simple wine". When three buckets of that were diluted by one bucket of water, *polugar* was the result. Anyone offered *polugar* could test its quality by pouring it in a metal container of about half a litre before setting the *polugar* alight. If burning reduced it to a line marked halfway down, it passed the test. It had a definite bread flavour, which gave rise to the term "bread wine".

The best vodka produced today is quadruple distilled and often advertised as ultra premium or super premium, although triple distillation, which began in the 18th century, is the typical standard for most vodka. The number of distillations is rather meaningless when it comes to judging the quality of a particular vodka but has become a way for vodka producers to imply that they undertake superior processing techniques.

Each country which produced vodka would use its own methods. Russian vodka is characterised by charcoal filtering, which began with the aid of birchwood in the 15th century. It continues today with charcoal, which has been prepared to make it porous. Raw spirit is diluted with water before being passed through the "activated charcoal" in order to remove impurities and oily deposits known as fusel. As we will see, this is an important feature that contributes to Russia's claim that it distills the "only true vodka".

Long before vodka came to Russia, alcohol decided which religion the emergent nation should follow. In 988, Vladimir I, the Grand Prince of Kiev, heard all of the arguments for Judaism, Islam and Christianity. Because Jews had no land and Islam forbade alcohol, Vladimir adopted the Eastern Orthodox faith and declared, "Drinking is the Joy of the Russ", a remark that has reverberated down the centuries as a commandment that must be obeyed.

Most countries which have become associated with a particular type of alcohol are able to date with accuracy when it first appeared. Whisky, Scotland's "water of life", was recorded as being in production in 1494. Although vodka and Russia are always considered to be Siamese twins, there is no surviving evidence of exactly when vodka production began in Russia or even if it was invented there. These questions arose when a trade dispute between Russia, Europe and the United States in 1977 centred around a precise term to describe the spirit. Poland was also a claimant to the vodka throne, and both countries, supposedly Communist allies, scrabbled around in their archives to find supporting evidence for their respective claims.

Russia and Poland launched an official historical search to resolve the argument, and in 1982, Moscow declared that vodka had been established in Russia by the 1430s. Happily for the Soviet

Union, an international tribunal concurred and declared Russia to be the inventor of vodka. The researcher W. W. Phoblehkin, a famous food historian who unearthed the evidence, turned his conclusions into a book on vodka. He was later found murdered in his suburban Moscow apartment. It was maliciously suggested that he had been targeted by a Pole, but the crime has never been solved and appears to have been without motive.

To decide when vodka appeared in Russia, the researchers looked at other alcoholic beverages that were commonly drunk, such as mead and beer, to see if anything had affected their production. A disruption or discontinuity might have encouraged the creation of a substitute and would offer support to the traditional story that vodka was invented by an enterprising Moscow monk around the 1430s.

Something akin to vodka had been brought to Moscow by the Genoese ambassador in 1386, an *aqua vitae* (living water) distilled from grape *must*, but it was not manufactured anywhere in Russia. As *aqua vitae* was a Muslim invention, its properties were often considered medicinal rather than for direct consumption, and it was used in the preparation of perfume.

Russia was awash with adulterated mead in the early 14th century, and the consumption of this inexpensive, watery and vinegary concoction infused with narcotic herbs "enjoyed" by the masses was slowly declining.

Beer was brewed domestically and collectively, especially in rural areas, but the Church regarded this as a pagan cult activity because a "March beer" was brewed to celebrate the pagan new year on the first of that month. The new year was moved to 1 September in 1424, and the Church abolished all beer brewing. There was suddenly nothing left to drink that could also match beer and mead for cheapness.

Ironically, the Church accidentally filled the gap. During a visit to Italy at the end of the 1430s, a Russian Church legation was probably shown stills operating in monasteries. An educated monk called Isidor was one of the representatives. His sympathies for Rome, expressed during the trip, offended the Grand Prince of

Moscow, Vasily II, who imprisoned Isidor on his return to Russia in the Chudov Monastery attached to the Moscow Kremlin. In the year before he escaped to Kiev, Isidor had an unusually comfortable incarceration, and his enforced leisure allowed him to experiment in distilling alcohol by using rye, which was readily at hand. It was an inspired choice, for grain was in abundance and the "water of life" was produced with an estimated proof of 60 per cent. Two centuries later, the proof was between 15–20 per cent and was drunk in larger quantities.

Isidor has since been appropriately immortalised in a new vodka from Russia called Legend of Kremlin, which includes his name and the year of 1430 on the paper-break seal on the bottleneck.

Vodka was tailor-made for Russia as it did not freeze like other alcoholic drinks in sub-zero winter temperatures and its quality did not deteriorate so it could be kept indefinitely. The financial reward against the outlay of material and labour was magnificent.

It is possible that a second visit in 1426 by the Genoese, again bearing *aqua vitae* to the Russian court, made more of an impression than it did before and may have suggested the idea of vodka to Isidor. Some sources suggest that the court did not drink the Genoese *aqua vitae*, but as alcohol was already a feature of Russian life, it seems unlikely. Talk and the taste of the strong liquid from Italy may have lingered in the good monk's memory and encouraged his experiments in the monastery. For Russia it was a piece of good luck when it was decided that the *aqua vitae* from Italy was a harmful potion and its importation was banned. Nothing could now compete with vodka and nothing would do so.

Distillation spread to other monasteries but was confined to those in the Moscow region, and in 1474 a state monopoly on the sale of vodka was imposed by Ivan III. As only the state could sell vodka, the spirit became the state treasury's chief revenue provider, an indication of vodka's popularity even then.

The Church initially resisted Ivan's pressure but was finally forced to give up selling vodka in 1478. When vodka later became responsible for widespread drunkenness, the Church conveniently had a memory lapse about its part in creating what it called "the devilish poison". Since no monastic records of the birth of vodka survive, the Church could not be accused of hypocrisy and certainly not by a merry drinker who was admonished by a Russian priest with the words that his greatest enemy was vodka. "Really," the drunk replied, "and does it not say in the Scriptures, 'Love thine enemy?'"

Although vodka was firmly established in Russia at the end of the 15th century, its vast empire lay in the future. Emergent Russia was ruled by tyrants. Poor Vasily II had been blinded by a cousin in a typical example of the savagery inflicted on family members during endless succession struggles. But the ruling power of the grand princes of Moscow increased as they acquired more and more territory in neighbouring lands. The capital was removed from Kiev and established in Moscow, and Ivan III felt confident enough to take the title of "tsar" for himself. A second marriage in 1472 to the ugly and grossly fat Sophia, a niece of Constantine XI, enabled Ivan to incorporate the Byzantine double-headed eagle as part of his insignia. The eagle, familiar to present-day vodka drinkers, more than compensated for the bed that his hefty wife broke when she arrived in Moscow.

Ivan, whose stern, angry gaze made women quake when they saw him, often fell into a drunken sleep during dinner. But aware that his fondness for alcohol was shared by the peasants, he banned all drinking except on high days and holidays because drunkenness interfered with their work.

The rapid spread of vodka did not go unnoticed by foreign visitors to Russia. As early as the 1470s, the Venetian ambassador to Moscow considered the Russians to be:

> ...great drunkards and take a great pride in this, despising abstainers... Their life takes the following form: they spend all morning in the bazaars until about midday, when they set off to the taverns to eat and drink; it is impossible to get them to do anything afterwards.

Both the Venetian ambassador and Giles Fletcher, sent by Elizabeth I of England to negotiate trade with Russia, commented on what became known as *kabaks* or "the tsar's taverns". These were established by Ivan the Terrible in 1552 and became as much a part of Russian life as the pub would for the British. The Moscow *kabaks* were at first only for the use of *strel'tsy,* the palace guard, to whom Ivan granted special drinking privileges whilst charging the tavern owners for the licence.

Fletcher spotted a tsar's tavern in every large town that he visited. It seemed to him that "to drink [to become] drunk is an ordinary matter with them every day in the week". The peasants would arrive with all their money and not leave until the last kopek was spent, Fletcher reported. It was not possible for one woman to drag her husband out of the tavern, as he was drinking for "the honour of the emperor".

The German scholar Adam Olearius, who was on a trade mission to Moscow in 1634 on behalf of Frederick III, Duke of Holstein-Gottorp, recorded an unintentionally amusing account of Russia. He noted that there were over a thousand of the tsar's taverns in which women appeared to have no shame about being drunk. In Narva, he spotted several women who:

> came with their husbands to a carouse, sat with them, and drank amply. When the men had got drunk, they wanted to go home. The women demurred, and though their ears were boxed, nevertheless, they declined to get up. When at last the men fell to the ground and went to sleep, the women sat astride them and continued toasting one another with vodka until they, too, became dead drunk.

According to Olearius, it was common for drinking couples in the tavern to indulge in sexual intercourse in front of sniggering spectators, and men and women thought there was nothing wrong in exposing themselves when lying on the filthy floor.

Priests and monks practising an abstemious life within sanctified walls would make the most of outside hospitality, and after a visit to the tavern, they were often found drunk and lying in the street. It was a situation that was so common that it evoked no comment.

There were drunks of all classes including the Grand Ambassador who, when sent to the King of Sweden in 1608, drank too much of a particularly fiery vodka and died on the day he was to have been received by the king.

Clearly it was perfectly acceptable to be drunk in public in Russia as early as the 17th century, and no behaviour was ever considered too gross. Olearius decided that Russia was the drunkest nation in the world, but it is difficult to believe that he only sipped water while sitting in the tavern. He noticed that not only money but garments were taken in payment for vodka in the taverns:

> In Novgorod, I saw such besotted and naked brethren come out of the nearby tavern, some bareheaded, some barefooted, and others only in their nightshirts. One of them had drunk away his cloak and emerged from the tavern in his nightshirt; when he met a friend who was on his way to the same tavern, he went in again. Several hours later he came out without his nightshirt, wearing only a pair of underpants. I sent for him to ask what had become of his nightshirt, who had stolen it? He answered, with the customary 'Fuck your mother', that it was the tavern keeper, and that the pants might as well go where the cloak and nightshirt had gone. With that, he returned to the tavern, and later came out entirely naked. Taking a handful of dog fennel that grew near the tavern, he held it over his private parts and went home singing gaily.

Such drunken behaviour and sexual depravity flew in the face of all Christian teachings, and the increase in loose conduct can be directly traced to the ready supply of vodka, always plentiful in the network of taverns. The Church preached against drunkenness and immorality, but the country's dependency on vodka tax revenues was such that the keepers of the tsar's taverns were told by the state "not to drive drunkards away from the tsar's taverns under any circumstances". The peasants felt that they could behave as they liked, since the Church did not stop them. In any case, the local priest was often to be found enjoying a drink with them, although it was forbidden for clergy to buy spirits.

Despite Olearius's rather jaundiced view of others drinking vodka, he was pleasantly surprised and impressed by the welcome he was given by a count in Moscow in 1643. Hosting a grand dinner, the count told Olearius that the greatest honour a guest could be shown was the presenting of the host's wife after dinner. By tradition, she would not dine with the men but would offer the guest a cup of vodka "from her own hand" in another room:

> Before we left he brought his wife and one of her relatives to meet us; both had young, lovely faces and were richly dressed. They were accompanied by an ugly attendant, the better to emphasise their beauty… after a sumptuous dinner he called me away from the table and the other guests. He ushered me into another room… then his wife came forth. She had a very lovely, but berouged face, and was dressed in her wedding costume. She was accompanied by a maid who carried a bottle of vodka and a cup. Upon her entry she bowed her head first to her husband and then to me. Then she ordered a cup of vodka poured out, took a sip, and handed it to me to drink, repeating this procedure three times. Then the count invited me to kiss her. Since I was unaccustomed to such honours, I kissed only her hand, but he insisted that I kiss her mouth. Accordingly, out of respect to a higher ranking personage, I was obliged to adapt myself to their custom and accept this honour. Finally, she handed me a white satin handkerchief, embroidered with gold and silver, and embellished with a long fringe.

Aside from the revelry that went on inside the *kabaks*, the premises themselves become notorious danger spots, attracting thieves and others who were ready to take advantage of the drunks.

For almost a hundred years since Ivan created the tsar's taverns, successive rulers legislated either to increase or reduce vodka sales, generally reversing the actions of their predecessor in a pattern that would recur to the present day. When a decline in the quality of vodka precipitated a peasants' tavern revolt in 1648, it was quickly suppressed by Tsar Aleksei Mikhailovich. Aware that the business of both distilling and selling vodka had become a complete mess, the tsar convened a special assembly known as the "tavern congress" in 1649 to revise the vodka regulations. The result was the twenty-fifth chapter of the "Code of Tsar Aleksei Mikhailovich". It was the first law ever devoted to the trading and distilling of vodka and an indication of just how important the spirit was to Russia.

Ironically, the entire peasant class of Russia had itself contributed to the poor quality of vodka because many peasants were too drunk to sow the wheat crop during the previous Easter. They were often heavily in debt to the local tavern keepers who were themselves involved in bribery and corruption.

The change of law forbade the sale of vodka on credit and closed down private, and therefore illegal, taverns. The staff of the tsar's taverns were replaced if they were at all suspect, and any illegal sales were punished by a beating and imprisonment to reinforce the fact that the commerce in vodka was a royal prerogative. Nevertheless, the system slowly broke down towards the end of the 17th century when the *kabaks* were rented out to individuals who were allowed to make a profit. The notorious *kabak* would change its name from time to time through the centuries, but the "tsar's tavern" would in essence remain the same and be the only place where vodka was legally available to purchase.

At the beginning of the 18th century, Tsar Peter I was revolutionising Russia and founded the new city of St. Petersburg in 1703. It was said that Peter I drank twenty glasses, or two litres, of vodka each day, and his contribution to both its abuse and acclaim as a drink would be legendary. The Scot Patrick Gordon, who was a general in the Imperial Russian army, noted in his diary that the thirteen year old tsar handed him a *charka* of vodka when the general was about to visit England, and they both probably drank a toast to his safe return.

What though, was this mysterious "devilish poison" like in the 18th century? Distilled vodka was colourless and almost odourless, and since it could be made on tavern premises, the distillation method was necessarily fairly simple and did not require complex equipment. Later, potatoes, rice, and in the 20th century sugar beet and molasses, would be used to make vodka, but the spirit was initially made from rye. When the rye was mixed with water, it resembled a kind of porridge mash. Yeast was then added, and the mixture was heated on a stove in a pot shaped like an inverted cone from which a long pipe fed the drops into a flask. Once the boiling point of alcohol was reached at 78 degrees Celsius, the alcohol would evaporate off into the flask as vapour.

The taste of vodka was disgusting and unpalatable due to its crude filtering, and was cloudy in appearance. To make it drinkable, herbs, spices and honey were added to disguise its foul taste. Each tavern keeper would have his own recipe, as the flavouring was *ad hoc* and depended on how well the crude vodka had been prepared.

The licentious behaviour of the peasants drinking the vodka and the general backwardness of the nation were often commented on by Europeans who could not believe that an early medieval society could still flourish in the 17th century. Moscow, then the largest city in the world and full of ramshackle wooden buildings, was frequently ravaged by fire. It was hidebound by superstition and had a class system that was incomprehensible to an outsider. Best seen from a distance, the city shone when the sun lit the golden-domed cathedrals and rich palaces of the Kremlin.

A closer examination would reveal dark, filthy streets that were thronged with robbers and murderers. Many inhabitants dozed off on their way home from an excess of vodka and froze to death overnight. Each morning, the police brought the corpses found in the night to a field for identification by relatives. When it rained, the mud and clay were so soft that it was impossible to go outside without sinking into the swamp. The only refuge was found in the tavern and the temporary escape vodka provided.

Foreign eyes might wonder at the city's clutter of contradictions. But looking down on his native city from his vast height of six foot and eight inches, Peter I did not like what he saw. Full of contradictions, Peter was a prodigious drinker and both the Jekyll and the Hyde of vodka. It was a dual role that could only be expected from one whose frequent, kind and sensitive actions seemed incompatible with his zeal in beheading over two hundred of the Moscow *streltsy* regiment, which had rebelled against him. Stalin described his reign as "a singular attempt to jump out of our country's frame of backwardness", while Solzhenitsyn saw only "a man of mediocre, if not savage, mind".

An enthusiastic traveller from an early age, Peter came to England in 1698 where he was offered lavish hospitality by William III. He preferred to go about London under a false name, but Peter's hopes of wandering the capital in anonymity were unrealistic, as his unusual height attracted attention.

Peter sublet the diarist John Evelyn's house with a door that opened onto Deptford Dockyard where he learned about ship building. Peter explored London, learning how to repair watches as well as observing how coins were made at the Royal Mint by a new method.

On his days off, Peter and his party slowly wrecked the house. Evelyn's butler complained that the house was packed with nasty people and just how nasty was only discovered when Peter left after three months. The wreckage surveyed by Evelyn and his friend Sir Christopher Wren included floors so stained that they had to be replaced as well as battered paintwork and smashed windows. All of the fifty chairs in the house had vanished, having probably been converted into firewood. Particularly unfortunate was the flattening of a thick nine foot-high hedge planted by Evelyn forty years earlier. Wheelbarrows, then unknown in Russia, were raced with a man inside, including Peter, and rammed into the hedge. He would later use the same method of transport to convey barrels of vodka at his garden parties in Russia.

Full of the ideas and customs of Europe, on his return to Russia, Peter proved adept with scissors which he himself used to cut off the boyars' beards – to him, a ludicrous appendage on the faces of his state counsellors. Those boyars who insisted on keeping their beards had to pay a tax and carry a metal token to prove it had been paid. He reduced the length of flowing sleeves and long trailing garments on anyone who wore them, including women. Peter's plan to westernise Russia began with these gestures but culminated in his construction of St. Petersburg in just ten years. By moving the capital there, Peter I showed the world his contempt for the old order and Moscow itself. He had vodka sent out to those who were laying the foundation of the city as they worked waist-deep in the swamp land he had chosen for St. Petersburg.

Amongst the first buildings to be completed was a tavern, the "Triumphant Osteria of The Four Frigates", where Peter "used to refresh himself with his favourite beverage of vodka spiced with cayenne pepper". Peppered vodka perfectly complemented the spicy food Peter preferred, while his sense of humour matched that of a governor of Moscow who trained a bear to hand vodka round to guests. If they declined, the animal would remove their garments one by one, starting with the hat.

When Peter was in Paris in 1716, he complained in a letter to his wife that, "There is an appalling situation. I have only one bottle of vodka left and there is none, absolutely none, to buy in Paris. I don't know what I'll do." It was said that a peasant who saved Peter's life was given the right to drink as much vodka as he wanted from any distillery. Afraid that the tsar's document granting this would be stolen when he was drunk, the peasant asked Peter to stamp his throat with the Imperial seal instead. This is the supposed origin of the gesture of tapping one's chin or throat to indicate a desire for vodka.

Peter the Great's own enthusiasm for drinking began at 18, when he became a member of The Jolly Club, an organisation which existed for harmless fun. This included walking in the countryside and knocking on the doors of noblemen before demanding food, shelter and drink. If the full membership turned up, about 200 had to be catered for.

The Jolly Club was gradually transformed into The All-Joking, All-Drunken Synod of Fools and Jesters where Peter served as a deacon of a mock church. The tsar despised the Orthodox Church because of its power, and the church regarded him as the anti-Christ.

The tsar saw no shame in making a false copy of the Gospels, which opened to reveal vodka bottles instead of Holy Water in readiness for mock baptisms. Perhaps the most notorious of his own ceremonies was the wedding he organised for an elderly, lecherous mock patriach and a buxom widow of thirty-four. This happy day began with a long visit to one of the tsar's taverns, while the four messengers sent to invite the guests were stutterers. The bride was attended by infirm old men, while the footmen, who were supposed to run on ahead, were the fattest men that could be found. A cart of musicians was drawn by roaring bears, and the wedding, with all the participants drunk on vodka, was blessed by a deaf and blind priest.

The drunkenness that is associated with Peter was not confined to The Jolly Club and its successor. He gave generous parties which were an ordeal for the guests. Constantly watched by the guards, they could not slip away unnoticed. Peter gave a new meaning to being "royally entertained" and regarded any party he gave as a failure if everyone did not leave drunk.

At the tsar's Peterhof Palace, guests were forced to drink until they literally dropped, but more alcohol would follow. Peter would produce the "Great Eagle", a crystal cup which held 1.25 litres and was filled to the brim with vodka. Downing it in one gulp, often in front of a laughing audience, was one of Peter's favourite punishments for anyone who had upset him. (The cup appears to have been lost, although it gives its name to a painting, *The Grand Eagle Cup* by Valentin Serov, and features in Pushkin's incomplete *Peter the Great's Blackamoor* in which the cup is filled with malmsey.)

One party of guests in 1715 were spared the "Great Eagle" only to be commanded to chop down clumps of trees for a path to the seashore, with Peter himself swinging an axe. When the woodsmen had finished, they returned to the palace for supper during which they drank “such a dose of liquor”. Instead of reviving them, it sent the guests “senseless to bed”.

Only an hour and a half of sleep was allowed before they were dragged off to visit a neighbouring prince who plied them with wine and vodka until four in the morning. None of the guests remembered how they managed to go home, but the relief must have been indescribable. It was short-lived, for the party was not yet over.

Summoned to breakfast at eight, the guests were supplied with vodka in lieu of tea and coffee. The day only ended after they were then soaked to the skin when a storm blew up as they sailed to the naval island of Kronstadt, which was nineteen miles from St. Petersburg. The rough crossing, which lasted seven hours, had the useful effect of sobering up the passengers, but when the boat landed, there were no beds where the merrymakers could rest. The partygoers had to strip naked and dry their sodden clothes by a fire, while they were wrapped in sledge covers lent by peasants. There was some consolation in the fact that Peter, who had cheerfully left his guests to look after themselves, caught a fever on the following day.

A description of a Petrine party in St. Petersburg in 1721 by Frederick Bergholz, the son of a general in Russian service, is peppered throughout with the word “whisky”, but it is clear from the context that vodka was being described. Bergholz’s account is extremely important because it is the only account that describes vodka of early 18th-century Russia in detail:

> Presently came several evil apostles, inspiring almost everyone with dread and alarm; I mean a half dozen or so grenadiers of the Guard, who, in pairs, were carrying on hand-barrows basins of the commonest grain alcohol, which gave off such a powerful odour that many sensed it while the grenadiers were still in another walk, more than a hundred paces away… many people immediately fled as though they had seen the

> devil… we began to run with all our might… I met several men who complained bitterly of their misfortune in being unable to get the taste of [vodka] out of their throats… one conscienceless rogue knew how to verify whether I had drunk or not and asked me to exhale. I replied that it was useless since I had rinsed my mouth with water, to which he retorted that I should not tell him such a story; he knew that nothing would help; 'even though you put cinnamon or cloves in your mouth, for not less than 24 hours the mouth would smell of [vodka] all the same, and you would not get rid of the taste for a still longer time'…

Exactly why vodka had become nearly undrinkable by 1721 was probably due to several changes in government control. Desperate for instant funds in 1705, Peter had rented or farmed out the state monopoly to individuals who had to pay rent in advance. But they were often scoundrels who produced low-grade vodka. Although efforts were made to change this, it took time for the quality of vodka to improve. Peter himself contributed to a modification of the pot-still design and encouraged the use of charcoal for filtration.

The first monster of vodka, Peter the Great was also the first vodka king. In his latter guise, he made vodka socially acceptable at court, and with the royal seal of approval, it could be enjoyed every day, for it had been endorsed "by the highest in the land".

As a vodka monster, with the grotesque "Great Eagle", his "Drunken Synod" and a court that was never sober, Peter used vodka as a political weapon against his enemies, including the Church. His fondness for the spirit was aped by others who thought excessive drinking the norm. When glasses were raised to the three hundredth anniversary of the birth of St. Petersburg in 2003, a new vodka was launched called *Zarskaya*, or The Tsar's Vodka. Fortunately, it does not resemble The Tsar's Madeira, a nickname for low-grade vodka.

After his death, Peter the Great remained a formidable presence who made his immediate male successors' achievements seem insignificant. His grandson, Peter III, is remembered chiefly for what he drank on each of the 186 days he reigned, according to the Moscow Vodka Museum. His wife, the future Catherine the Great, made sure that his drunken excesses would forever blacken his name. It is likely that she arranged the murder of her husband. Catherine was more famous for her fondness of acquiring young lovers and her vast size than for heavy drinking.

It was not Catherine but her predecessor, Elisabeth Petrovna, who has to be thanked for officially christening the spirit when, on 6 June 1751, the word "vodka" appeared in state papers for the first time. (It would not officially re-appear until 1900.) Its use came in the announcement of a new law, "Who is to be Permitted to Possess Vats for the Distillation of Vodkas", which saw Elisabeth allowing nobles to distil vodka.

In 1786, Catherine II ended state interference in vodka-making by passing an act which granted "to the Gentry in Perpetuity the Permission to Engage in Distilling", making it possible for the vodka industry to develop into large-scale production much later. Excused from paying tax and duty, the gentry distillers had to promise to produce vodka only for their personal and household use, and not indulge in the vulgar act of trade. One of the more unusual members of the distilling gentry was the English Duchess of Kingston who became a supplier of vodka on her estate.

The duchess had married bigamously and should not have used her title, but she continued to do so when she fled abroad as a widow with a vast fortune. She had bought an estate near St. Petersburg which she hoped to develop. Her plans failed, although the remnants of the distillery remained until as late as the Russian Revolution.

Landowners were now free to improve the quality of vodka, with serfs employed to do the hard labour. All of the raw materials for vodka including firewood came from the gentry's estates, and although the yield in proportion to materials used was about two per cent, the cost was minimal.

It has been calculated that to produce 20 litres of good quality vodka, the distilling process required:

> 1,200 litres of mash containing 340 litres of grain and rye malt and 12 litres of beer yeast to produce only 3.5 buckets (42 litres) of good "simple wine". Redistillation of these 42 litres, with the then obligatory addition of about a bucket of milk, gave a maximum of 15 litres of good, pure grain spirit... [A third of water was then added to complete the process.]

Some distillers tried to infuse the spirit with flavourings of vegetables, herbs, fruit or berries to represent every letter of the alphabet. This was an imaginative task, especially as the Russian alphabet then had about 40 letters (reduced to 32 after the 1917 revolution), and some even aimed to produce two or three vodkas for each letter. One such distiller's list, in Russian alphabet order, included:

> *Anisovaya* (aniseed), *Beryosovaya* (birch), *Vishnyovaya* (cherry), *Grushovay* (pear), *Dynnaya (*melon), *Yezhevichnaya* (blackberry), *Zheludyovaya (*acorn), *Zveroboynaya* (St John's wort), *Kalinovaya* (Gilder rose), *Limonnaya* (lemon), *Myatnaya* (mint), *Malinovaya* (raspberry), *Nogotkovaya* (cowpea), *Oblepihovaya* (sea-buckthorn), *Polynnaya* (wormwood), *Pertsovaya* (pepper), *Ryabinovaya* (ashberry), *Smorodinovaya* (currants), *Tminnaya* (caraway), *Ukropnaya* (dill), *Fistashkovaya* (pistachio), *Hrennaya* (horse-radish), *Cheryomuhovaya* (bird cherry), *Shalfeinaya* (sage), *Schavelevaya* (sorrel), *Estragonnaya* (tarragon), *Yablochnaya* (apple).

From this evolved a genteel party game amongst the nobility. Vodkas were poured for each letter of a word which had to be guessed from the different vodka flavours.

Catherine II's main contribution to Russian vodka history came not in the change she made to vodka laws, but the improvement in the quality of vodka itself. She boasted about the fine vodka with justification and sent bottles of it to some of her correspondents including Voltaire who, as a wine connoisseur, was likely to be a severe critic. When asked if she was afraid that her gift would earn a sarcastic comment from him, Catherine is said to have replied that the philosopher would swallow his tongue out of surprise, delight or envy for Russia. Unlike Peter, Catherine disliked drunkenness and drew up a list of rules that her guests were expected to obey, including: "To eat of the sweet and the savoury, but to drink with moderation, that each may always find his feet on going out of the doors."

Another friend who received a present of vodka was the Swedish botanist, Linnaeus, who was so overwhelmed with the spirit that he wrote a pamphlet on its wonderful qualities, parts of which were extremely useful for later advertising copy:

> This drink has a magical power. It strengthens the weak and revives those who have fainted. Those tired after work and physical activity can return their life forces by this drink much sooner than by nourishment… It works as a diuretic, an appetizer, an anti-toxin…

Vodka was now appearing in popular books of engravings of Russian daily life. One published in 1765 showed three gentlemen seated at a table and being served vodka by the wife of one of the men, with the doggerel verse as explanation:

> The wife herself in days of yore,
> Serving, to the table bore
> A glass, to cleanse the taste,
> Of vodka each one's lips to baste
> To make them eager for the feast.
> And as she held the tray for each,
> She offered every guest a kiss.
> Such a custom's worth our praise,
> I'd only one objection raise.
> I know what swells their ardour –
> The good wife's kiss will scent their lips,

Their teeth will smell of vodka sips.
But if your wife is plain my friend,
Then serve the vodka at the end.

Illustration for the doggerel verse above 1756

II

Russian Daily Life in Vodka

> The church is near but the road is icy. The tavern is far but I will walk carefully.
>
> *Russian saying*

Visitors to Russia never ceased to be surprised that they seemed to see vodka wherever they turned. In the early 19th century, vodka-fuelled celebrations in the cities were just as lively as in the country. The joy of religious festivals were not hindered by any false piety. The conclusion of Divine Service to celebrate a feast day in August in the Donskoi Monastery in Moscow was "the signal for general mirth" which witnessed the congregation rushing outside to the "immense, circular, and elegant *Votki-Tents* " full of:

> numerous great copper pots or tubs, filled with *votkii.* The persons employed to sell this nectar of the day can scarcely answer the demands of the crowd, who, according to the quantity they purchase, receive it in a larger or smaller unglazed shallow, earthen vessel, for which a deposit is given till returned… Then come quarrels and abuse: drunkenness, rolling and tumbling usually conclude the day. Such a fete is a perfect Russian scene… As soon as the twilight approaches, the police interdict the sale of *votkii*; but when the weather is fine, great exertions are required to disperse the crowd, so that it is eleven or twelve o'clock at night before the curtain drops.

The bowls were probably made of pottery due to the scarcity of glass in Moscow, a problem not affecting St. Petersburg. At a summer festival in the latter, some tents sold vodka wholesale in large square bottles, but "in general it was doled out in small measures, the purchaser spilling a portion into a tub as the perquisite of the waiter."

The backwardness of Russia compared to western European nations was highlighted by its defeat in the Crimean War. The tsar and the nobles ruled over a largely primitive and illiterate peasantry which formed four-fifths of the population. The living conditions for that vast majority had hardly altered since the reign of Peter the Great.

The stop-start and confusing system of farmers and merchants retailing vodka under state licence had resulted in several peasant tavern revolts. From the end of the 18th century through to the 1850s, vodka found in the taverns was often watered down two or three times and did not measure up to the 40-50 per cent pure alcohol volume that it was supposed to contain. To encourage the peasants to drink even this, the accompanying food was spiced up with pepper and salt to make them even thirstier. The absence of fixed closing hours offered further impetus to consume more.

The profit to the farmer-retailer was as much as 100,000 per cent of the cost of production. By the 1850s, the highest earning vodka farmers were making as much as 80 million roubles in profit per year. (One rouble in 1850 has been calculated as having roughly £10 of purchasing power in today's Britain.) The high price of the spirit, and its adulteration with anything from poisonous weed to soap and copper deposits, encouraged smuggling of cheap vodka from outside the easily controlled regions.

The government did nothing to stop the vodka farmers, for as the minister of finance commented in 1810, "No other major source of revenue enters the treasury so regularly and punctually… its regular receipt on a fixed day of the month greatly eases the task of finding cash for other expenditures."

Nothing had changed by 1826 when a government statement

expressed hope that the peasants would drink rather more than moderately. As Russia was suffering a decline in grain export, the only way it could benefit financially was if the excess grain was distilled into vodka. The state's "thirst for revenue [and] the peasant's thirst for forgetfulness" combined to make the vodka industry "Russia's most technologically advanced". This technological savvy was buttressed by new types of stills and production techniques from western Europe that had been imported to Russia by the early 19th century.

A traveller from California, used to the widespread drunkenness in the state's bars, felt quite homesick when in Moscow in 1867 and wrote affectionately that, after the sobriety he had observed in most of continental Europe, it had cheered him up when he saw bearded peasants drunk and enjoying vodka:

> Of all the traits I discovered in the Russian people, none impressed me so favourably as their love of vodka… I admired their long and filthy beards and matted heads of hair… but in nothing did I experience a greater fellowship with them than in their constitutional thirst for intoxicating liquors. It was absolutely refreshing, after a year's travel over the continent of Europe… to meet at every corner of the street a great bearded fellow staggering along blind drunk… There was something very congenial in the spectacle that greeted me on the very first day of my arrival in Moscow.

Even if visitors did not like vodka, they could at least be grateful that the mention of the spirit was almost a holy utterance, so instantly could it lubricate a difficult request. Vodka was demanded by each new coach driver on a journey of any length and was not begrudged in the severe winter conditions of Siberia. It was essential for travellers to be able to say the phrases "I will give you vodka money – *Damn na vodku*", and "I won't give you vodka money – *Nedam na vodku*". Both statements were included along with the Polish equivalent in the useful phrases of *Murray's Handbook for Travellers in Russia,*

Poland and Finland, published in 1865. The writer George Sala found "*Damn na vodku*" indispensable when he was in Moscow and St. Petersburg, but to him, vodka tasted of "bilge-water, vitriol, turpentine, copal-varnish, fire, and castor oil".

The obligation to drink vodka to mark every significant event in the average Russian's life was never questioned, least of all by the peasants who could ill afford the quantities required for a good celebration. At every event in village life, vodka was always the main guest and the last to leave. A Russian peasant interviewed in the 1860s remarked, "we drink the damned vodka at weddings and christenings, at funerals and church holidays, when receiving guests, at every purchase and sale, on going to the market and at meetings... on every occasion."

It was suggested by some observers that if the peasants could enjoy "more civilised forms of entertainment, such as balls, concerts, and literature" instead of overindulging in vodka, they would "escape the burdens of their dreary lives". In the meantime, the peasants had to forego the pleasure of the ballroom. Instead, there was near-complete acceptance of widespread drunkenness amongst the peasantry as well as town dwellers.

In the 1830s, an inspector looking at the way peasants lived in a Russian province noted that children began to "drink at an early age and continue all their life. Their parents give them vodka with bread, and they soon acquire a taste for it and begin to drink it in large quantities." The best time to start them off was at the end of September on Michaelmas Day at harvest time when everyone in the parish got drunk. The inspector complained that, "Everyone drinks – the young, the middle-aged, and the old; the men and the women." In the taverns, both sexes were "drinking together with abandon and often forgetting about the children they have left at home with a crust of bread."

When work requiring a communal effort was needed, such as road-making or help with the harvest, whoever needed labour, known as *pomoch*, could not expect the workers' assistance without the offer of vodka – despite the fact that the work would often drag on or not be well done because of the resultant drunkenness:

> *Pomoch* is inconceivable without vodka. The work begins with vodka, continues with vodka, and ends with vodka… If you do not give the peasant plenty to drink, he will work poorly out of annoyance; if you do, he will work poorly because he is so drunk…

Just how much vodka would be doled out was fixed by local tradition. When the work was finally finished, the employer invited everyone back the next day to celebrate its completion and to finish off any drink that might have been forgotten. Everyone involved, from the young to old grandmothers, came along to the party.

If an offer of cash was made instead of vodka, it was usually turned down, for the communal working scheme meant that when individual workers needed similar help, they would expect it to be reciprocated. If there was any skimping on the quantity of vodka, the temporary employer would be cold-shouldered by everyone.

Being part of the *pomochi* and showing that they were old enough to drink and take part in an adult world was a rite of passage for young men who thereby demonstrated their independence from their families. They had to learn how to hold their drink and, as a result of conversations with seasoned older drinkers, they became part of the village network through which they could hear about opportunities to work. If they were lucky, they could also learn about the local women available for marriage.

In fact it was at weddings that the greatest amount of vodka was drunk, and it was not uncommon for the bridegroom to provide six to eight vedros of vodka – a vedro is 3.249 gallons of U. S. standard measure, or 2.706 imperial gallons – which was all drunk before the wedding. The cost of the wedding celebrations fell on the bride's family, which might spend as much as two hundred roubles on vodka. It was a colossal expenditure for poor peasants to find – but found it had to be. In the winter, a wedding guest arriving late for the wedding breakfast discovered that:

> Everyone had already regaled themselves well. Many lay unconscious in the street with uncovered heads and were buried in snowdrifts as the wind covered them with snow… In another place, I saw them put a senseless drunk on a sledge, tie him to it, harness his reindeer to the sledge and drive off… The bridegroom himself was lying among the completely drunken guests. Even the bride, a child of 13, was already drunk.

The Church was not forgotten either, and the priest's fee for a wedding, apart from cash and food, was three bottles of vodka. The rural parish priest was often as drunk as his parishioners, as depicted in the painting of 1861 by Vasily Perov, *Easter Procession in a Village*. He owned nothing and, like the peasants, had to work in the fields. For him:

> …the epitome of pleasure is to fraternise with the peasants in noisy, wild drinking bouts; with joy he sets off to the tavern, drinking house, whatever – just so he is invited; if they do not invite him, he will unabashedly go and get senselessly drunk with a friend from his parish.

Not all priests were drunks or even willing drinkers. During religious festivals, the local priest would process through the village bearing an ikon. He would be obliged to call on every house, where he would be offered food and vodka. Declining the offer often resulted in the whole family falling to their knees and refusing to stand up again until the priest drank some vodka. If the priest refused once more and then walked out, leaving the still-kneeling family, the host would be furious, and there could be problems later on. If the priest approached the peasant to ask for help, he risked a tongue-lashing for his perceived lack of respect in the past. But if the priest drank the vodka to be tactful, by the time he had called on every house, he would be unable to utter even a simple prayer.

Tradition demanded that young men who were conscripted to join the army would go on a tavern crawl for weeks in advance of leaving home. If their money ran out, they would take the last kopek from their family, else they would be considered dishonoured. Smashing windows as they rampaged through the village, the revellers would play the accordion and sing all through the night. They were tolerated with good humour – if anyone asked what the racket was, the explanation dissolved any anger. More dangerous were the drunken celebrations at Lent when the villages were invaded with relatives, with some of the arrivals falling off troikas while others plunged into deep water ravines. During one celebration, a vodka soak was swiftly dispatched when unable to move quickly enough away from a wagon that tipped over and crushed him to death.

Those who were not conscripted into the army did not lose out from the chance to take part in heavy-drinking sessions, which spontaneously erupted during street parties. Illegal moonshine called *samogon* was sold from a stall, often by an enterprising old widow, which saved the drinkers the walk to the tavern. Visits to friends were only considered a success if there was a good supply of vodka, but there were few complaints if there was little to eat.

The first grain from the harvest would be taken to the miller to be ground. It was celebrated with vodka in exchange for some of the grain. The landowner, needing workers to take the grain to the market, would also treat them to liquid refreshment. Occasionally the workforce was reduced due to fights in the fields at harvest time, which saw scythes proving to be fatal weapons.

Those harvest workers who overcame such dangers would start working at sunrise and come home for breakfast. On the way back to work, the peasants would drop in at the local tavern for a few vodkas and repeat the visit after dinner and supper. Holidays and Sundays would also involve a quick trip to the tavern as part of the journey to Mass. After a rural christening, which normally took place at about eleven o'clock in the morning or at noon, participants would go back to the house. A typical scene was described as follows:

> Vodka is served immediately. The average peasant provides, depending on the harvest, from one bottle up to five pints of vodka and even more if he is the type that does not pass up an occasion to get drunk and, at the same time, happens to have extra money to spend on liquor. The hosts offer drinks first to the godparents, and only after that to the rest of the guests. If the vodka is plentiful, everyone gets drunk. But songs are not sung, as this is not appropriate at a christening dinner. The new mother is also in attendance, but, because the christening usually takes place the day after the delivery, she stays removed from the crowd, resting on a bench in the back of the room. The newborn wails. The guests joke around. When the baby makes too much noise, they say [to the mother]: "Hey, you little cow, where did you hide your teats?"

Visitors' censorious accounts of Russians' drinking habits were rarely challenged, but an Englishman in St. Petersburg, W. R. S. Ralston, a noted folk-tale researcher and translator of Turgenev – having heard mainly from his fellow countrymen about "the drunkenness of the lower classes" – decided to investigate the subject for himself and form his own opinion. He was "always on the lookout for drunkards", but after spending over six weeks in Russia, he did not see as much drunkenness as in London, nor as much violence.

Nevertheless, Ralston went into several, mainly "women only", pubs, bringing a plainclothed police officer with him for safety. In one unnamed city, they descended some steps into dingy vaults where Ralston was struck by the number of poorly-dressed women he found there. They were friendly despite being "horrible to look at". He invited them to join his table and sent for their "favourite liquor… the horrible *vodka,* or coarse whisky, which is sold at about three half-pence a tumbler."

A token effort was made to provide a basic version of *zakuski* with the vodka, which arrived "with the black bread which always accompanies it, cut into little cubes, and sprinkled with salt". They went into another tavern and climbed up some rickety stairs. By groping their way in the dark and by feeling the damp and greasy wall, they found themselves in a half-lit attic with almost no furniture beyond "a tottering table and two or three paralytic chairs".

Despite the fact that the women became maudlin in their conversation, they were never nasty, but explained that they were driven to the taverns because of poverty. One woman confessed that "she was so given to drink that, even if a place were found for her as a servant and she were able to keep it for six months without reproach, the seventh would be sure to see her back here again."

It was not until 1881 that the Russian government decided to make sweeping changes, which would involve replacing the dingy taverns, or *kabaks*, with inns that sold food to soak up the vodka. A completely new concept was to be introduced: off-licence sales would offer vodka in bottles in the hope that less would be drunk at home than in an evening at the tavern. Since the Middle Ages, vodka drinkers had been forced to take the spirit home in either a barrel or a bucket, and the measures inside the tavern were no less than one *charka,* or 150 ml.

The premises selling off-licence vodka were purposefully unfriendly and contained no furniture so that it was impossible to sit down to drink any purchases. A note of religious devotion and patriotic loyalty was to be introduced with the result that the walls had to be hung with pictures of saints and the tsar. A grill was to separate the tavern keeper from the customer, who had to leave the premises immediately after paying.

The concept of bottled vodka had never previously been mooted as Russia lacked a good glass factory, and although bottled vodka could be found in Moscow and in St. Petersburg, the spirit was usually put in old wine bottles.

When the bottles were manufactured for vodka, many had a green complexion, which may have contributed to the nickname for vodka of "the green serpent". The creation of vodka bottles meant that distillers could "brand" their vodka on a label, and many of the new labels were strongly pictorial to help the illiterate remember which vodka they liked. Pyotr Smirnov, the son of two illiterate peasants, made sure to sell his standard vodka in distinctive, light blue bottles.

Smirnov's firm made bottles shaped like bears for its strongest vodka, while other containers took the form of elephants and busts of the tsar. Smirnov also created a unique bottle shape for a rowanberry vodka that became particularly popular and was instantly recognisable. As vodka had not yet been officially named, the spirit was often confusingly labelled as "table wine". (In Poland, the bottle itself was a cause for confusion. The use of vodka there had often literally been medicinal, and the typical vodka bottle resembled something found in the medical chest where it could be discreetly hidden amongst less appealing mixtures.)

But the introduction of bottles and the revised law made very little difference to the drinking habits or the lack of sobriety of those who had drunk vodka in the taverns. They might be called "inns", but they were still used as taverns, for the habit of drinking by "the lower classes" without food had become ingrained. When quarter bottles of vodka were available, the contents were often quickly drunk outside the off-licence door in order to recover the deposit on the bottle without delay.

Because taverns were such a central feature of Russian life, they were a popular subject for painters. *Morning at the Tavern* (1873), by Leonid Ivanovich Solomatkin, cheerfully depicts a small crowd freezing in the winter snow and waiting for the tavern to open. Many are clutching large kettles to take the vodka away. It is past opening time, and an old soldier checks his watch while a man thumps on the door. They are all longing to be let in. *The Last Tavern at the City Gates* (1868), by Vasily Grigorievich Perov, displays a bleak scene in which a frozen woman sits on a horse-pulled sleigh while a dog shivers nearby in the deep snow. She waits for her husband to leave the warm tavern and return home with her.

The ridicule of the foreigner that was heaped on the vodka-soaked Russians in the *kabak*s often showed a misunderstanding of the function of the village inn. There was no other building in the community where the locals could meet to conduct business or hear about local activities. Large gatherings outside of the tavern were forbidden and in any case, it was often too cold to talk in the open air. The tavern was the only place where the locals could read a free newspaper, meet travellers with news from beyond, buy from travelling salesmen and where strangers could mix with the local inhabitants. All village business was concluded in the tavern with a vodka toast. The glass had to be full to the brim up to the moment of quaffing and could not be sipped. To show the glass really was empty, tavern dwellers upended it and proclaimed "*Postai*".

The tsarist officials were often suspicious of what was said there, for the tavern was usually a safe haven from officialdom. They might have been filthy and insanitary, but the Russians made the taverns "something like free churches, or open debating societies". The tavern was later described as "the secular soul of rural Russia".

From birth to death, every breath inhaled seemed to reek of vodka. In the case of the executioner, vodka fumes would be exhaled on those about to breathe their last. One of the bonuses of the executioner, himself a prisoner, was the right to demand a free shot of vodka from every tavern passed on the way to the place of execution. Unsurprisingly, the journey would be arranged along the most provident route. For the executioner, it was a cause for joviality and he would generally throw back the vodka with an obscene joke. The vodka seller would make the sign of the cross and smash the empty glass to pieces.

The habitually large volume of vodka drunk by the peasants was also the result of the spirit having been watered down. It had acquired a few nicknames from the peasants themselves, such as "Thinner than water", "Oh to be drunk!" and most frustrated of all: "Scalds the tongue but leaves you sober". In 1859, peasants attacked the taverns and drink shops in protest at the diluted vodka that they were drinking, and those individuals caught were sent to Siberia. Old problems of the past had returned, and it was found that many farmers responsible for supplying the taverns had diluted the vodka by fifty per cent with water. In some cases, they had also included tobacco, narcotic herbs and belladonna to make it intoxicating.

But the situation was soon to change as a result of social reforms introduced in the 1860s by Tsar Alexander II. Serfs – peasants owned by the state, the aristocracy and landowners by hereditary right – were granted their freedom. The reform had a massive impact on the vodka industry and would in due course lead to the foundation of the House of Smirnov.

Zakuski

III

The Official Birth Of Vodka in 1894

Not long after the introduction of the vodka reform in 1863, the government discussed introducing changes to control the quality of vodka. The ministry of finance enlisted the help of the Russian scientist D.I. Mendeleev who had researched alcohol-water solutions. Famous for publishing the periodic table of elements, but less well known for bigamy and his expertise in making leather goods, Mendeleev was asked to devise a system in which vodka would be measured metrically and not by weight.

He advised that the government should insist on testing vodka by alcoholometry – the method of determining the proportion of pure alcohol in spirituous liquors. This would not only improve the standard of vodka but would ensure uniformity of the base product in all distilleries.

At last it seemed that something would be done to eradicate the adulterated, low-quality vodka that had flowed unchecked for centuries. Changes were slow, but by 1884 a scientific committee of the nation's foremost scientists supervised all research on vodka and quality testing. A Distiller's Congress had also been investigating the varieties of vodka-based drinks and commented unfavourably on fruit-flavoured vodkas known as *nalivkas*. Its report listed the harmful chemicals found in them and noted that, "this slush is poured into bottles with beautiful labels... Then it is baptized with names such as raspberry *nalivka* and sent... to all ends of Russia."

This was one of several veiled comments aimed at Smirnov, and many such flavoured vodkas were found by the report to have had alcohol contents reaching just twenty-four per cent whilst also being laden with fusel oil – an impurity that was already illegal. This was eventually eradicated when the monopoly distillers were legally required to use one pound of charcoal to filter every bucket of vodka.

Working towards the changes that would be introduced when the vodka monopoly was implemented, the government had agreed to accept the result of Mendeleev's experiments on water and alcohol. A biographer of Mendeleev is at pains to state that the scientist did not invent the formula for vodka of forty per cent proof, as is often suggested, but that his experiments confirmed that this was the result of triple distillation. When adding the pure vodka spirit to an equal weight – rather than an equal volume – of water, the actual liquid volume was reduced to forty per cent. This is because when water and ethyl alcohol mix, strong hydrogen bonding draws the different molecules closer together than in a pure solution, resulting in a loss of volume.

Mendeleev also insisted that as the spirit would consistently have the same alcohol content no matter where it was purchased, it should be known throughout the Russian Empire as "vodka". The various names that had been used for vodka types, such as "bread wine", "grain wine" and "Russian table wine", would become redundant.

The committee investigating the state of alcohol in the country found that the cost of making vodka was extremely cheap. A bucket of vodka would sell for more than six roubles, but the cost, even after taxes were paid by the distiller, amounted to less than half of the price. With the government anticipating such profits enhancing the state treasury instead of enriching the distillers, nothing would stop the monopoly, but it could not be introduced overnight. Initially introduced in the provinces and later in St. Petersburg and Moscow, the measure was enforced across the country by 1902.

Not only was the standard alcohol content fixed at forty per cent proof, but only rye was to be used. Potato-based distillation was cheaper but messier and, it was claimed, did not suit the distilling plants, which had been adapted to process Russian rye.

Using local Moscow soft water and eschewing any added

flavouring, the "monopoly vodka" set a new standard of vodka purity. It was the vodka by which all others were to be judged. The vodka spirit would continue to be distilled by private distillers, but other changes would include bottling vodka in sealed, tamper-proof bottles to guarantee its quality and purity.

The brief for implementing this change was given to Count Sergei de Witte, the minister of finance, who intimated that the idea came from Tsar Alexander III himself, supposedly out of concern for his intemperate subjects. Witte related in his memoirs that he had enforced the monopoly throughout most of Russia by 1903. But there was naturally a great deal of opposition and well-founded suspicion that the monopoly was introduced to expand the exchequer rather than reduce vodka drinking. Witte toured the vodka distillers and told them that the success of the monopoly would be judged, "not by the amount of income derived by the state from the monopoly but by the beneficent effect of the measure upon the morals and health of the people…"

He did not fool the *Anglo-Russian News*, a supposedly pro-tsarist paper published in London. In 1897 it commented on the vodka monopoly and what it regarded as the easy manipulation of a drunken nation by autocracy:

> The Russian minister of finance has presented to the tsar a glowing account of the beneficial results of the working of the government monopoly of the liquor traffic when… the revenue to the crown from the sale of spirits, has practically doubled, trebled, and, in some provinces, even as much as quadrupled… Such a government as the Russian cannot possibly dispense with vodka without endangering its very existence… Vodka renders an actual practical political service… as long as the [peasant] is obedient, the official can command… Where vodka is altogether or nearly absent, there you will also find the tsar's authority shaken and general prosperity developed.

The peasant in Russia contributed more in indirect tax than the lower orders of any other country in Europe, and the government's financial optimism was justified in 1900 when it was calculated that sixty per cent of Russia's revenue came from vodka. By way of comparison, the revenues from oil and gas production accounted for fifty per cent of the Russian state's revenues in 2012.

The disastrous Russo-Japanese war of 1904–1905 instigated the slow crumbling of Imperial Russia and the shaking of the tsar's authority. Bolstered by vodka, the soldiers were often drunk during battles. Although it was probably an exaggeration, a temperance worker stated that, "The Japanese found several thousand Russian soldiers so dead drunk that they were able to bayonet them like so many pigs." A field-doctor more reliably reported that he saw "masses of aimlessly wandering soldiers, red-eyed from alcohol, dust and exhaustion, surrounding an official from the quartermaster's office who ladled vodka from a huge barrel to anyone who wanted it."

What was described as "the great vodka debauch" occurred during the Russian retreat from Mukden:

> The vodka casks were hacked open with knives, swords and axes, attracting an orgy of men who pushed and crowded in, trying to swallow the gushing vodka with their mouths, or to catch the spirit in any container they could grab, including empty sardine tins and even the cases of the Japanese shells… The vodka that overflowed collected a foot deep in a depression in the ground. Men knelt down to drink the muddy liquor, scooping it up in the hollows of their hands as one would scoop up water from a well. Some fell into it bodily. Many were wetted by the jets of liquor from the barrels squirting over them. Buriat Cossacks, Mohammedans from the Caucasus forbidden by their religion to touch drink, riflemen, dragoons and every other sort of military person joined in this mad spree. With the dust and the smoke from the burning stores eddying around them, they looked like alcoholic demons struggling in the wreck of hell.

Part of the problem lay in soldiers' entitlement to a daily ration of vodka. Even regular officers were forced to drink under the threat of dismissal. For the soldiers, vodka was a central part of their lives, whether on or off the battlefield. After the reports of the drunkenness that featured in the Russo-Japanese war, distribution of vodka in the army and its sale in soldiers' shops was prohibited in 1908.

Witte's successor as minister of finance died shortly after assuming office and was replaced by Vladimir Kokovtsov, who was desperate to raise revenue to fund the war. According to Witte, Kokovtsov "distorted the meaning of the reform". Now that the government needed vodka to produce as great a profit as possible, "no police measures were taken against drunkenness" in order to encourage the consumption of vodka.

The price of vodka was increased, which had some effect on "habitual consumers but not so high as to render the vodka inaccessible to the masses". But when the war ended, the government campaign continued to promote the sale of vodka. A disgusted Witte noted that the number of vodka shops had doubled. Faithful to Alexander's memory, he wrote reprovingly, "It was the minister's duty to remember the late emperor's original purpose in carrying out his vodka reform..."

At the same time as war was being waged with Japan, hunger and discontent raged amongst the lower orders of Russian society. On 22 January 1905, a peaceful workers' march in St. Petersburg was fired on by troops and erupted into a nationwide revolution. Relaying the carnage, *The Guardian* reported the looting of a government vodka shop where £320 of vodka was destroyed and the area was strewn with the wreckage of broken glass.

The unrest grew in momentum such that Russia was almost closed down by strikes in October. The navy and army were mutinous, and revolutionary parties were attracting new recruits. Witte was appointed prime minister and gained Nicholas II's grudging acceptance of the demands contained in the October Manifesto, which called for the *duma* to be allowed to assemble, civil rights including the freedom of speech and progress towards a universal franchise. But the unrest continued into the next month when four government vodka distilleries and the imperial glass factory went on strike, and Witte's appeal for law and order was ignored.

Despite having negotiated a brilliant face-saving settlement to end the Russo-Japanese conflict in September 1905, Witte was dismissed from government service a few months later by his furious royal master and replaced by the reactionary Stolypin.

Witte noted of Stolypin's views and policies that, "Men and women, adults and mere youngsters are executed alike for a political assassination and for robbing a vodka shop of five roubles. Sometimes a prisoner is executed for a crime committed five or six years previously."

Ironically, when four drunk extremists arrived at Stolypin's house to make an attempt on his life, they failed due to an excess of vodka. Two came disguised as policemen escorting a "prisoner" with the assistance of their "coach driver". While they were talking to the doorkeeper, a bomb fell from the helmet of one of the assassins and exploded, killing two of the terrorists. The grounds of the house were strewn with fragments of bodies, pieces of clothing, watches and uniforms. In the house itself, the remaining walls and plaster were spattered with blood and fragments of the victims. A witness stated that he saw "three bodies without heads and a heap of almost unrecognisable flesh and clothing".

"Stolypin," *The Guardian* reported, "was saved by the would-be assassins having drunk numerous glasses of vodka which they had imbibed on several evenings in order to lull suspicions while maturing their preparations." The following evening, as foreign journalists tried to explain to their readers why the Russian government was so hated, a correspondent for *The Observer* bought two bottles of vodka to encourage an interview with a soldier on night-sentry duty. The soldier told him that he had a deep distrust of the tsar, whom he regarded as a coward hiding away from his troubled people: "A man of no mind or no will, who cared nothing for the thousands and thousands who were killed through his worthlessness."

Stolypin's daughter suffered the amputation of both of her legs as a result of injuries from the bomb. He was later shot dead in 1911 while viewing a performance at the Kiev Opera as he sat next to his "worthless" master, the tsar.

Promoters of the vodka monopoly had stated that it would reduce crime, but it was found that the monopoly encouraged illegal distillation. Meanwhile, drinking in public resulted in hooliganism. A commentator wrote in 1905 that, "Drinkers who previously remained hidden in various taverns and 'dens of drink' now exhibit their vice on the streets, which cannot help but have a harmful effect on the public."

In St. Petersburg, drunken youths walked in broad daylight along the Nevski Prospekt and thrust pornography into women's faces, fluttering the pages as they went. One spot in the city became notorious because two drunk masked men dressed in black would frequently leap out of the bushes to startle passing women. Other youths drunk on vodka removed the bolts from park benches and stood by jeering and laughing when those who sat on them collapsed to the ground. A man who regaled the passengers on a tram with a song before trying to press vodka on a woman had his bottle grabbed by two other drunks. Perhaps surprisingly, they did not drink the vodka themselves but instead forced the contents down the singer's throat.

An official government temperance department, known as the the Guardianship of Public Sobriety, had been established at the same time as the introduction of the monopoly law. For obvious reasons, the department recommended moderation rather than complete abstinence. Various incentives to give up vodka drinking were promoted in St. Petersburg and Moscow. Reading rooms, amusements and entertainments were offered in the main cities to those who signed the pledge. Most remarkably, a new church was built in St. Petersburg in 1908 for the city's temperance movement, "The All-Russian Alexander Nevsky Society of Sobriety". Built next to a large slum area, this Church of the Resurrection of Christ was constructed without central pillars to maximise space and may have been paid for by a one-kopek temperance tax that tavern owners had to pay for every ten roubles they took from alcohol sales.

In the provinces, stories akin to religious testaments were told of how peasants previously ruined by vodka had mended their ways, saved and bought horses and were leading contented lives. It was not what the government wanted to hear, especially when rural areas were allowed to control vodka sales and had shut down seventeen taverns in Ryazan. Governors of other Russian provinces then vetoed similar attempts in their fiefdoms, and the rural temperance movement slowly died.

The October Manifesto so grudgingly signed by Nicholas II had removed some restrictions on civic meetings. This made it possible for a conference known as the "First All-Russian Congress on the Struggle against Drunkenness", which met in late December 1909 and continued into early January. The conference was a disaster. Instead of discussing alcoholism in Russia, some members of the conference ranted against the tsar for reaping a vast financial harvest from the vodka monopoly at vodka-drinking peasants' expense.

Vodka had never been absent from any aspect of Russian life, and as the First World War approached and more peasants came to live in the cities, their beliefs that devilry rather than vodka was responsible for their domestic crises were half-jokingly exposed in court reports. Vodka featured in student magazines as the subject of silly jokes: "Alcoholic: a man who drinks vodka on only two occasions: when he has herring and when he doesn't have herring." On the Russian stage too, a glass of vodka was the symbolic shorthand that instantly summed up the drunk stock character that often featured in comic operas and plays, thereby rendering lengthy explanations redundant. Vodka in Russian life was as ever present as air.

But with a few strokes of the imperial pen, vodka supplies would be reduced by the state monopoly before being prohibited – less than ten years after vodka had been officially created and given its name.

Warning signs of trouble came early in 1914 when Sergei Witte, the architect of the 1894 monopoly, spoke out against his creation. He had always intended that the reform would be a control against drunkenness, but instead, "the suppression of alcoholism was pushed to the rear, and the object of the monopoly became the pumping of the people's money into the government treasury." By neglecting the evils of alcoholism, a new evil had arisen, "...the so-called 'Hooliganism'. Hooliganism is a legitimated child of alcoholism."

The death rattle in the throats of vodka drinkers began in February 1914 when the tsar, after seeing the results of vodka on households for himself – "tragic scenes of the degeneration of the people, the poverty of families, and the decline of households as a result of drunkenness" – sacked his minister of finance who had been urging the sale of vodka. Nicholas II told his new finance minister that the state would have to exploit other resources and issued an edict to that effect.

If there was any doubt about the wisdom and necessity of once again revising the vodka laws, it was banished when reports circulated in St. Petersburg that the vodka shops, closed for three days at Easter, were mobbed after they reopened. As a result, twenty thousand arrests for drunken behaviour were made in one day.

Over the next six months, at an enormous cost of lost jobs, distilleries were closed, vodka shops were shut down and the state vodka monopoly was ended by order of the tsar. Specially-designated policemen went round all of the nation's vodka outlets and locked up the supplies, which were then secured by the Imperial Seal.

The end of the monopoly cut the entire national revenue by £90,000,000 – more than a quarter of the government's income. *The Guardian* speculated that the peasantry, "so habituated to drink", would find it "highly improbable that they could accept such a drastic reform". The newspaper reported that in 1913 the peasant class had "consumed no fewer than 283.5 million gallons of spirits – an increase of 24 million on the figure of the preceding year". The paper quoted figures stating that there were 2,983 vodka distilleries in Russia in 1912 and that the state owned and managed 28,016 drink-shops. Adopting a rather censorious tone, *The Guardian* reminded readers that:

> It must not be forgotten that the Russian drink-shops only sell spirits and must necessarily exercise a more deteriorating effect on public health on account of the much lower consumption of food by the Russian peasant and working-class masses… the quantity of vodka sold in Russia was… nearly nine times as large as spirits sold in the United Kingdom in the corresponding year.

When Russia entered the First World War, the revenue from the former vodka monopoly was no longer there to help finance the war machine. Worse was to come when Nicholas II astonished the nation by stating on the 4 September that the sale of spirits would be prohibited for the duration of the war, an example which was copied by the other European nations fighting in the war.

It was not in the character ofNicholas II to pay attention to anything his people wanted, particularly the peasants, and the increasing unrest of the people was matched by the tsar's determination to stamp it out. The *duma* could be rendered powerless by the tsar's ability to overrule laws he did not like. The ruinous effects of vodka, due in part to the state monopoly, had been raised in the *duma* by Michael Chelysev, the Samara representative. He claimed that the results of drunkenness, such as frequent wife beating, starvation and poverty, could be wiped out if local councils were allowed to accept the petitions of teetotal-minded peasants to shut down local drink-shops and taverns. According to his own account, he was received shortly afterwards by the tsar in the Crimea: "He was impressed with my recital that most of the revolutionary and Socialist excesses were committed by drunkards and that the navy revolts and other mutinous movements were all caused by inebriates."

According to *The Guardian*, the tsar sent a telegram on 20 October to the Association of Peasant Teetotallers announcing that it was "the tsar's firm will to abolish for ever in Russia the sale of spirits by the state".

Socialists who had attacked the tsar for creating the monopoly and enslaving the peasants to vodka found that its removal had robbed them of a useful propaganda weapon. Instead they now complained that prohibition interfered in personal liberty.

The vodka prohibition was a well-intentioned decision, but possibly the most fatal to be made by Nicholas. Along with the First World War, its ramifications contributed more to his abdication and assassination than anything else. This may seem an exaggeration, but the influence of the green wine would be felt beyond falling revenues due to prohibition.

The First World War was a disaster for Russia. In its desperation for money, it printed more, which led to inflation. Everyday necessities, especially food, soared in price. The country's military failure, which was apparent after one year of conflict, would lead to widespread dissatisfaction amongst its troops.

The only cheerful reports were of a reformed peasantry. *The Guardian* newspaper informed its readers that "the 'green serpent', as the drink habit is called by the Russian peasant, is defeated". The newspaper reported that the country was, "in the unanimous opinion of the Russian press, celebrating the grandest victory in the present war". Effusive accounts of the vodka ban resulting in lives reborn and rich prosperity were published throughout Russia. According to a village priest, the closing of the drink-shops amounted to a:

> transformation, which has overtaken our villagers... They are all now better dressed, industrious, more sensible. It is a pleasure to see how one of the 'weak men', who always used to go about drunk and would carry to the public house the last sack of flour or the last dozen eggs from under the hen, is now putting up a new gate at his courtyard and passing the evenings in the company of his wife who had for years never been free from the traces of his fists, discussing with her various household things rendered possible by a new superfluity of money. All, without exception, are only wishing that the sale of drink may never be renewed.

Almost six months later, *The Guardian* reported that the astonishingly positive effects of vodka's absence were still being maintained. The difference to the prosperity of rural families was significant. One peasant woman, wanting her own happiness to be known, asked a country newspaper reporter to write on her behalf that, "We were poor. But then, when my man gave up drink, we bought hens and a cow."

The same newspaper confidently noted that: "By one of the greatest reforms in the history of the world – great because it has achieved the greatest results in the shortest time – a nation of 150,000,000 souls has passed as it were in a night from the empire of vodka into the empire of light."

It all seemed too good to be true, and it was. There were rumours that vodka was being served in certain places in teapots, and in some districts there were reports of cases of poisoning from "turpentine, eau-de-cologne, methylated spirits, children's balsam and other 'medicinal mixtures'".

Once it was realised that vodka really had gone and there was no end to the war in sight, many peasants in rural areas became increasingly gloomy and fed up. They found that celebrations had become boring without vodka. Weddings were badly attended for the same reason and were as "merry as funerals". Tea proved to be an inadequate substitute. In one province, godparents were hard to find for baptisms, since the traditional presents of vodka had been abolished. Funerals were also harder to arrange now that payment could no longer be made in vodka for coffins or the digging of graves.

The unkindest truth about vodka to infuriate the peasant was that it could still be had during the prohibition. It was available at restaurants, which paid a high price for the licence to sell vodka, and was consequently a preserve of the rich. Although fruit vodkas could be bought because the state was anxious to encourage the growth of fruit markets, the alcohol content was fairly low.

While many peasants were desperate to find vodka, by early 1916 the *duma* was equally desperate to find ways of disposing of the vast amount, some 260 million gallons, that lay in storage. The minister of finance had been accused of keeping it stored in order to sell it once the war was over. He declared categorically that: "The government will encourage temperance after the war. A return to the old state of affairs is impossible." Instead, the government announced that vodka would be used in combination with benzine for motorists, and longer opening hours would be granted to traders who used it for lighting. Most novel of all, the ministry would fund a factory to manufacture artificial india-rubber from vodka. (In fact some years before the war, Britain had bought fusel oil – the unwanted by-product found at the end of vodka distillation – from Russia to use in its own artificial rubber.)

Sensing revolution in the air, the aristocracy were having what would be a last, desperate fling with privilege by indulging in champagne and caviar parties. They sang a popular song which indicated how even they could not find ready supplies of vodka:

> We do not take defeat amiss,
> And victory gives us no delight
> The source of all our cares is this:
> Can we get vodka for tonight.

By this time, the monarchy would only survive for another year, but the process of decline had already started when Rasputin was murdered in December 1916. Exactly how Rasputin managed to control the haemophilia of the tsarevich will never be known, but his constant contact with Nicholas and Alexandra became the subject of damaging gossip and rumour, which was even portrayed on the stage.

It was said that Rasputin had been constantly drunk on vodka and that the poison administered in his drink by his assassins was slow to work because he had a high vodka tolerance. Rasputin was under constant observation by the Russian secret service for months before he died. The amount he drank and his frequent drunkenness, were duly noted, but what he actually drank could not be monitored. The secret service could only observe him from a distance, as it did not wish to arouse suspicion by entering premises that Rasputin lived in or visited. On the morning of 10 August, following a wild party the night before, vodka is given only this mention:

> Rasputin came out of his house… sighing and wondering at having got so drunk, since, according to his own words, he had had only three bottles of vodka. He repeated over and over again: "Ah, my dear fellows, that was an ugly business."

Rasputin's admission suggests that he was capable of far more in the way of vodka consumption than three bottles a night. The spirit was not produced on the night of his murder, and the poison which failed to work was dropped in his sweet madeira, thereby masking its taste. If Rasputin had drunk vodka, he would probably have detected the taste of poison at once.

More startlingly, however, is recent evidence that his murder was organised by the British secret service and that the fatal shot was fired by a British agent. The British government was afraid that if Rasputin's constant pleas to the tsar to withdraw from the war succeeded, the Allies would be vulnerable to a build-up of German troops on the western front.

The inflation brought about by the depleted, vodka-less tax base and the subsequent printing of paper money meant that the peasants were unwilling to sell their grain on the open market. Although they were paid high prices for it, the money they received lost value with every passing minute. Instead, they preferred to dispose of the grain locally, and only small amounts became available for city use. Much of it was used for making the infamous *samogon*, which had become a useful bartering tool for goods that were in short supply. Grain that should have been in surplus was not reaching Petrograd, as St. Petersburg was now called.

Peter the Great's city was difficult to keep stocked with fresh supplies, marooned as it was on the Baltic coast, and food could not be readily transported there because many of the trains previously available were reserved for the war effort. Bread was inevitably in short supply, and when bread queues were found throughout

Petrograd, it was announced on 19 February that bread would be rationed. Even when flour was found, a shortage of fuel to light the ovens contributed to the bread shortage. Strikes and riots spread rapidly across Petrograd with the rallying cry, "Give us bread". This was followed by, "Down with the government", and "Down with war!" The Russian revolution had begun and would last just ten days.

An attempt to protect the Winter Palace in Petrograd from the revolutionaries failed, and when it was stormed, the imperial wine cellars were looted. The palace was supposedly guarded by the top regiment, the *Preobrazhensky*, but this had been rendered uncommandable because of vodka-fuelled drunkenness amongst the troops. Countless replacement regiments were sent in as one after another became intoxicated. The looting only stopped when a Finnish regiment was brought in, which threatened to blow up the wine cellars and shoot the looters if the plundering did not stop.

Deprived of alcohol for so long, soldiers in Petrograd led a series of vodka riots which escalated into street battles. The Red Guard was assigned the task of protecting stores of alcohol but had to use an armoured car against their own men, killing three of them and eight soldiers from the Semenov regiment who joined the attack on the Petrov vodka distillery. Lenin, who had seized power from the Provisional Government, was not present at the storming of the Winter Palace in October, but he was disgusted to notice that soldiers who had attacked the distillery were licking up the vodka that was flowing on the ground.

He ordered that all marauders who tried to steal alcohol were to be shot, declaring that vodka was the enemy of communism. Orders were given for all of the Imperial stores of vodka and wine to be poured into the Neva. In the new capital, it was decreed that:

> All the stores of grape wine, cognac, flavoured vodka… are announced to be property of the Moscow Soviet of Peasant and Working Deputies… All the warehouses where these products are kept, all the equipment related to the industry, i.e. glass, boxes, covering material, dressing and fuel; also

> cash money in the wine-shops and warehouses belonging to the company and to [private persons] now belong to the Moscow Soviet of Peasant and Working Deputies.

It was a sobering start to a revolution.

The Provisional Government had declared that all grain including the produce of the harvest due in 1917 would be under government control and would be distributed via central government edicts. When the new Bolshevik minister of food reported that illegal vodka distillation was on the rise, the grain distribution was abandoned as there was no guarantee that it would be used for bread.

In March 1918 the Bolshevik government withdrew from the First World War and six months later, ordered the assassination of Nicholas along with his wife and children. It was the end of the Romanov dynasty.

A British Member of Parliament understood the situation very well when he stated in the House of Commons that:

> It is perfectly plain that if you interfere with the deep-seated social habits of a people, you will have an enormous disturbance, and that is what the poor foolish tsar did. He thought he had dethroned vodka and vodka soon dethroned the tsar.

IV

Soviet Russia

> Stalin belatedly discovered the virtues of vodka as an efficient social instrument to keep the proletariat subdued. The first industrial facilities to resume production, sometimes under direct artillery attacks, in the territories re-conquered from Nazis were – no surprise – alcohol distilleries.
>
> Nicholas Ermochkine & Peter Ilikowski, *Forty Degrees East*

The revolution and the collapse of Imperial Russia did not mean the end of prohibition. Vodka had reigned as the supreme spirit but was absent for ten years from the start of the First World War until its restoration in 1924. Lenin drank very little alcohol and was resolutely in favour of maintaining the prohibition, declaring that there would be "no trade in rotgut".

The only known conversation Lenin had on vodka was recalled by P.I. Voyevodin, later renowned as a film scriptwriter. Then one of the leading Bolsheviks in western Siberia, Voyevodin had come to Moscow in 1918 where he met Lenin for the first time:

> I told him about an occasion when there had been a big argument… over the problem of how to sell the vodka which had been stored in vast quantities in warehouses in Siberia. When the problem was discussed… some people, including me, suggested that we should sell the vodka to the peasants in exchange for grain. Only three Party members supported

> my suggestions. Ilyich said: 'The fools! What fools! You are in charge of economic affairs… Why didn't you push it through?' Then Lenin said: 'But could you have sold that vodka abroad?' I said that we could have kept France supplied with spirits for fifteen years. Then Ilyich asked, 'But could you actually get the vodka out?'… I told Lenin that we couldn't have transported it all down the River Ob [in western Siberia] because we didn't have the tanker barges or appropriate containers. What was more, in the lower reaches of the Ob, we'd have had to transfer all of it onto sea-going steamers. After reflecting, Vladimir Ilyich said, 'It's a pity you didn't sell it to the peasants. You should have ordered it. It ought to have been done.' I started to explain that it was not for us to decide to do it off our own bat. Ilyich said, 'If you'd done it, we'd have approved it.' I laughed and asked him, 'And then you would have condemned us?' Ilyich began to laugh, 'That's all right! We'd have condemned you for it, but you'd have done the right thing.'

It was believed that about a third of rural households were making *samogon* during the post-revolutionary prohibition years. The penalties for illegal distilling were very severe, including exile to Siberia, but the risk of being caught was less in the country than in cities. Nevertheless, vodka leaked into certain shops in Moscow where the coded request "for lemonade", along with a significant wink at the assistant, was perfectly understood.

Lenin had set up a "Commission to Combat Drunkenness" because he was afraid that if grain continued to be used for *samogon*, it might cause a bread shortage. The green serpent, which had consumed the tsar and brought Lenin to power, could rear its head and remove him. He reluctantly agreed for fiscal reasons to remove the prohibition in 1923 and instead control vodka through a state monopoly. But he did not live to see the change after dying in January 1924. Lenin's funeral was held on what proved to be the coldest day of the year. Ironically, vodka had to be given to the trumpeters to put on their mouthpieces so as to prevent their breath freezing on their lips.

He was succeeded by Stalin, who had no reservations about the necessity of the vodka revenue. At a party conference in 1925, he said:

> What is better, the yoke of foreign capital or the sale of vodka? This is the question facing us. Naturally we will opt for vodka because we believe that if we have to get a bit dirty for the sake of the victory of the proletariat and the peasantry, we will take this extreme measure in the interest of our cause.

Born in Georgia in 1879 with the cumbersome name of Ioseb Besarionis dze Jughashvili, Stalin, as he renamed himself, read Lenin's writings and became a Marxist revolutionary. He joined the Bolsheviks in 1903 and raised money for them by robbing banks. He became close to Lenin after the 1917 revolution, but the latter criticised Stalin in his *Testament.* The document was prepared not long before his death – an event hastened by an arrogant and insensitive letter he received from Stalin, which barely apologised for inexcusably rude remarks he had made about Lenin's wife. Lenin clearly expressed his wish that Stalin should be removed from the post of General Secretary and not succeed him. *Testament* was not made public, and Stalin would die in office in 1953.

It was joked that Stalin's father gave him a rag soaked in vodka to stop him howling as a baby, but he was never seen drunk and was rarely seen by the Russians. A virtual recluse, Stalin made very few public appearances.

He seemed to have enjoyed drinking heavily only with his close friends late at night, "mixing Georgian wine, brandy and vodka" and listening carefully for any indiscreet comments. He hinted to one colleague that his glass sometimes held diluted beer masquerading as vodka, which, resembling the brown-shaded *Okhotnichya* or "*hunter's vodka*" made by Stolichnaya, was flavoured with cloves, juniper, aniseed and coffee as well as black and red pepper. For maintaining the nation in a stupor, vodka was Stalin's most useful weapon in peace and in war. It was the familiar story of a drunken nation being easier to control than a sober one, but Stalin's reign was one of terror and control by fear.

As he increased his atrocities, making use of a network of secret police, Russia slipped back into vodka drinking as if there were no future, and for many there would not be. If anything, mass vodka drinking was greater than in the days of the tsar, with one commentator writing that "a wave of alcoholism engulfed the whole country". Everyone seemed to be drinking: "the well, the sick… adults… children… at celebrations… for appetite, for warmth and to refresh themselves."

Part of the problem with the return of vodka was that there were no longer *kabaks* to drink it in. As the taverns had been privately owned, most of them were now closed. Vodka could not be bought at bars or clubs and could only be drunk in restaurants or at home. It was available at workers' clubs, but for many the severe punishments for the pleasure of being drunk on vodka was not worth the risk of being caught.

A delegation of British trade unionists visiting Moscow in 1924 reported that vodka had been reintroduced at 20 per cent proof, half the strength of the spirit when last available in 1914. The weaker vodka was replaced the following year by the first Soviet vodka, which was 40 per cent proof and was informally known as "Rykovka" after A.V. Rykov, the chairman of the USSR. Moscow Vodka was reintroduced in 1925 and was the reputed favourite at the Kremlin. Its premises were developed from a former Imperial monopoly bottling factory, and despite the fact that the building was bombed by the Germans in 1941, it was appropriately used to make Molotov cocktails. It would later become the factory that continues to produce Kristall vodka.

There was no hesitation about buying vodka in Leningrad. The government released 180,000 gallons of vodka on the first day that prohibition ended and maintained a daily issue of 30,000 gallons to meet demand. Unfortunately, there were not enough bottles to cope with the quantity of spirit being produced despite all the bottle factories working overtime. The government ordered a nationwide increase in bottle production, requisitioning two hundred and fifty million bottles from just one factory.

For those peasants preferring a stronger vodka, *samogon* was often produced at 90 per cent. Thus a convivial evening drinking it at home would cost a third of the price of legal vodka. The production of *samogon* for "one's own use" was helpfully decriminalised after 1926. By 1928 greater standardisation resulted in 40 per cent vodka becoming the norm.

The end of prohibition had some unintended consequences for the Kremlin. The Russian Supreme Economic Council was cut off from the outside world for three months because one of its junior employees succumbed to a thirst for vodka. The RSEC supervised the work of state industries that were based in Russia and not the wider Communist bloc.

The task of stamping and posting the mail from that department was entrusted to one clerk, but the reintroduction of 40 per cent vodka proved an irresistible temptation to him. Unfortunately, he did not earn enough to satisfy his thirst, so he converted the stamps into cash, and the cash into vodka. He had a vague plan to buy stamps to post the growing pile of letters, but three months passed with the clerk still drinking away the department's stamp budget.

He failed to turn up to work for two consecutive days due to a massive hangover. By chance, a question about a letter was asked, and when the absent clerk's desk was searched, it was stuffed with the unposted mail. The most surprising feature of the clerk's lack of action was that all of the departments which were supposed to receive instructions in the unsent letters had functioned perfectly well without them.

After prohibition ended, traditional celebratory customs were resumed with gusto in the countryside. On one festive day, a family of eight living in a shack, was reported to have polished off 36 litres of vodka, a sheep and a pig with the aid of thirty guests. They had to live off bread, cucumbers and potatoes for the rest of the year.

Such regular occurrences stirred temperance societies into action with the result that in 1928, the estimated forty per cent of children who did not drink were encouraged to wave placards outside factories with touching appeals that read, "We demand sober parents", "Down with drunk fathers", and "Down with vodka". Less touching was the placard commanding, "Shoot drunks!"

Various temperance campaigns at the end of the decade were undertaken but were consigned to failure, partly because temperance activity did not suit Stalin at all. His solution was to merge the temperance movement with the anti-religious movement, "The Union of the Godless", along with the campaign to encourage the teaching of reading, known as the "Down with Illiteracy Society", into a composite body called "The Healthy Life Society". One of its magazine covers showed a modern version of Christ generously filling cups at the Wedding in Cana on a table cluttered with vodka bottles. Officially, alcoholism was no longer an issue, and as a state problem, it simply vanished.

In September 1929 Stalin wrote to Molotov, who was in effect his deputy, that it was essential for Soviet military forces to be increased. But he added:

> Where can we find the money? I think vodka production should be expanded... We need to get rid of a false sense of shame and directly and openly promote the greatest expansion of vodka production possible for the sake of a real and serious defence of our country.

He was opposed by Bukharin, a member of the board of the "Societies for the Struggle with Alcoholism". Stalin had him shot ten years later, while Molotov outlived nearly all of his contemporaries, dying at the age of 96 in 1986.

A propaganda film, *The General Line* by Sergei Eisenstein, appeared in 1929 and centres on a tough peasant woman who manages to persuade the hard-drinking male members of a commune to pool their money to buy a tractor instead of the vodka they would rather spend it on. The happy ending sees everyone working harmoniously together. In reality, the situation was dire because the peasants did not understand the concepts of communism, were unwilling to surrender the grain necessary for vodka and bread, and did not wish to work in collectives. The greatest suffering came in Ukraine where those who resisted Stalin's agricultural plans were left to starve to death.

Having seen off the temperance movement, vodka was an essential part of the 1931 Five Year Plan. But the spirit's ability to boost revenues meant that it was not cheap. The price had increased several times such that a two-third litre bottle cost four roubles, of which about three roubles consisted of tax.

Vodka retained its ability to make or break social interactions. Factory hands forced new workers to bring in vodka as part of their initiation rite and were shunned or given no instructions on how to work if they did not. But efforts to combat alcohol at the workplace continued. In some factories, models of cemeteries were placed near the doorway, with planted crosses clearly inscribed with the names of workers who were inefficient through drunkenness. If they did not reform their ways, the "habituals" were sent to rehab clinics.

Stalin's encouragement of others to drink vodka heavily in his company in the hope of careless talk was a triumph. The horror of having to endure an evening with Stalin could be mitigated by moderate vodka drinking, but too much was likely to prove fatal. Tomsky, one of his most loyal and trusted comrades, wagged a finger at his leader after consuming too much vodka, declaring loudly, "We'll find a bullet for you too." Not long afterwards, on learning he was to be tried for treason, Tomsky found a bullet for himself.

The evidence seems to suggest that Stalin never drank during a working day. If he had been a seasoned drinker, his air marshal, Alexander Golovanov, would not have been concerned when, during the Yalta conference, Winston Churchill initiated a vodka-drinking contest between himself and Stalin. Their glasses were refilled at an alarming rate, and those with Stalin were worried if he could keep up with Churchill, whose reputation as a heavy drinker was notorious. Stalin was holding his own, but when Churchill was carried away to have a rest, Stalin approached Golovanov and said: "Why are you looking at me like that? Don't worry, I won't drink Russia away. But tomorrow, he'll feel like a fish on a frying pan."

Stalin's nephew remembered a different state of affairs, recalling that his uncle "was in a state of collapse" after the Yalta Conference, where the "Churchill-Stalin vodka-drinking duel had been bad for him". But Stalin declared, "I don't admit his superiority even in the matter of how much alcohol we can take."

The two leaders had never enjoyed spending time together, and they had exchanged insults during their first meeting in 1942. Churchill sulked during the Kremlin banquet given in his honour, while the British chief of the imperial general staff, Alan Brooke, found that the minute they sat down, "vodka flowed freely and one's glass kept being filled up… During the first hour we must have got through at least a dozen toasts. Luckily, I had a jug of water in front of me, and when I was not being watched I filled up my glass with water instead of vodka."

Stalin's marshal, Kliment Voroshilov sent for a new vodka, which was coloured yellow and arrived in a jug with a large red chilli floating on the top. Brooke found it too hot to swallow: "It was just like drinking liquid cayenne pepper and completely choked up one's throat."

The Soviet marshal had no reservations about the pepper-infused vodka and drank two glasses in quick succession. Stalin deliberately waited until Voroshilov was drunk and, grinning broadly, walked round to his seat to propose a toast to him. Barely able to rise to his feet, Voroshilov gripped the table with both hands and rocked backwards and forwards, staring vacantly ahead:

> The critical moment arrived… Stalin held up his glass for Voroshilov to clink with. Voroshilov must have seen at least half a dozen glasses… he trusted to luck and lunged forward …Fortune was with him and he clicked the right one! Stalin walked off to fill his glass another dozen times for the other toasts, whilst Voroshilov with a deep sigh sank back on to his chair.

Stalin was remembered in a comic, grotesque and vodka-laden evening by William Christian Bullitt, the newly appointed first American ambassador to Soviet Russia in 1934 who was entertained with others by the Soviet minister of defence. The ambassador was completely unfamiliar with Russian customs, and his first surprise was the lavish banquet. After ten toasts had been proposed, the foreign minister Litvinov noticed that the American was sipping vodka from his glass. He told the ambassador quietly that "it was an insult not to drink to the bottom" and that he must do so. Bullitt managed the next fifty vodka toasts, grateful for having a head that was "impervious to any quantity of alcohol".

Stalin raised his glass to the "American army, the navy, the president and whole USA", while Bullitt toasted the continued success of the Soviet Union and the memory of Lenin. By this time the vodka clearly had gone to Stalin's head, a turn of events which must have chilled his deputy commissar for heavy industry, Georgy Pyatakov, a small and slight man who was a brilliant pianist. After marching him over to a piano, Stalin commanded Pyatakov to play, standing behind the hapless performer who was forced to launch into a series of wild Russian dances "with a manic furiosity at the keyboard, spurred on by Stalin's hands around his neck". Pyatakov was later shot for supposedly collaborating with the exiled Trostsky, charges which were subsequently proved to be false.

The hospitality was returned by Bullitt in a lavish party, which was later parodied by Bulgakov, one of the four hundred guests, in a chapter entitled "Satan's Grand Ball" in his novel *The Master and Margarita*. It sees champagne ruling during the evening, but vodka is provided as a restorative on the following morning.

It is claimed wrongly that the vodka brand "Red Army" was created especially by Stalin to give to his troops during the Second World War. Perstovka, a peppery vodka, was enjoyed by the Soviet army generals, but the vodka given out as a daily ration to the Red Army during the Second World War was Stolichnaya, which was not on general sale until much later. Superior to Moskovskaya, the vodka that had been made in 1894 and resurrected by the Soviets, Stolichnaya was created during the siege of Stalingrad when the state's chief distiller had time on his hands.

Stalin's reign was one of the longest Russia has ever seen, and through vodka he loosened the tongues of those close to him, and numbed an entire nation into submission. When he died in 1953, official mourning meetings were organised where the response was mixed. A Moscow carpenter remarked that: "I wish they had given us at least two hundred grams of vodka; then we would drink to the memory of the Leader."

Others felt that it was inappropriate to celebrate birthdays, drink vodka or laugh a few days after Stalin's funeral. When it was finally accepted that Stalin really was dead, some spoke their minds without fear of retribution. Brandishing a bottle of vodka, the leader of a tractor team from Rostov said to those present: "Let's drink to Stalin – to Stalin's death! Let's thank him for building a hundred and ninety thousand concentration camps for us."

Stalin was replaced and denounced by Khrushchev, who made a feeble effort to reduce vodka drinking. Poster campaigns were used by the Soviet government to warn against drunkenness and being "in the embrace of the green snake". Killing the dragon or snake was a useful image in various anti-vodka campaigns. Posters depicted the green serpent in its many evil forms, from strangling neglected babies in their prams to coiling around the bottles clutched by men as they drink vodka.

The most effective poster was also the simplest and became an iconic image of Soviet Russian art. A neatly-dressed young man, seated at a table with a rather unappetising meal of steak, peas and something unidentifiable on his plate, holds out a hand to reject a proffered glass of vodka. Simply captioned "No!" it is still reprinted as a postcard and a poster. It attracted an amusing riposte in the form of a near-identical poster in which a grinning Russian bear seated at the same table is offered a glass of vodka held in a pig's trotter, with the caption reading "Yes!"

Khrushchev tried to intoxicate Lester Pearson, the Canadian

foreign minister, and his entourage during a visit to Russia in 1955 by proposing countless peppered-vodka toasts. As soon as the glasses were empty, they were refilled at once. Perhaps out of historically-motivated spite, Khrushchev targeted a Canadian-Russian diplomat, George Ignatieff, who was the son of Nicholas II's last minister of education.

"I tried to spill some of the drink over my shoulder as I drained each glassful," Ignatieff recalled, "but Khrushchev immediately spotted my stratagem and announced that the 'count (or should I say ex-count?) was trying to cheat'." Ignatieff was pressed to, "Drink up like a Russian", which he did until he was violently sick during the meal. Khrushchev was so drunk that he had to be helped to his car by his bodyguards, but he sent a message to Pearson the next day, telling the minister that he was impressed by the way he had handled his vodka.

Khrushchev was a great fan of John Wayne and would watch pirated copies of the actor's films. During the Soviet premier's visit to America in 1958, he asked to meet the film star, and they met at a formal reception. They slipped away to a private room with a bar where Khrushchev told Wayne that he understood that the star enjoyed a drink. Wayne told him he had heard much the same thing about Khrushchev, and they discussed the merits of vodka versus Wayne's favoured Mexican tequila, drinking heavily as they chatted. A drunken Khrushchev babbled to Wayne via his interpreter that he was the leader of "the biggest state in the world and [I] will one day rule the world", to which an amused Wayne asked the interpreter to tell Khrushchev that he was "gonna knock him on his sorry fucking ass". This was tactfully changed by the interpreter, who told Khrushchev that Wayne "would buy him a drink the day he rules America".

The drinking contest was judged to be a draw, and when Wayne later received a box of premium Russian vodka with a handwritten note that read, "Duke, Merry Christmas, Nikita", he sent a special box of tequila to the Kremlin.

Khrushchev increased the price of vodka at the beginning of 1958 in an attempt to reduce heavy drinking. The press was bombarding the populus with anti-alcohol propaganda, particularly targeting late New Year revellers. Vodka was removed from films in which it appeared, and anyone shown celebrating a success by lifting a vodka glass was reprimanded.

Vodka addicts who were frequently found drunk in the street were rounded up and dumped in "drunk tanks", familiar to readers of Martin Cruz Smith's detective novels. It was quite a useful way to have free hospitality, for addicts were given a bath and coffee at the sobering-up stations and were allowed to sleep the vodka off before being released without any charge. The government half-heartedly targeted pseudo traditions such as workers spending their first wage on vodka. But when an anti-vodka campaign was given publicity in 1964, even the state's mouthpiece *Pravda* did not suggest that excessive drinking had stopped. The newspaper stated that: "The reasons for drinking have been eliminated – there is no poverty or unemployment."

The western world heard little of how Russian factories were in reality extremely unproductive, but the more amusing stories of vodka-related misconduct did leak out. A Soviet mother was awarded a "Heroine Mother Medal" for giving birth to ten children. Unfortunately it was discovered that the single mother had the children by ten different fathers and had packed off eight of them to a home. The two lucky enough to be kept with their mother were starved, while the generous family allowance helped the single mum to maintain a steady supply of vodka.

The succession of leaders which followed the bloodless coup that removed Khrushchev in 1964 made little impact on vodka over-indulgence until Mikhail Gorbachev came to power in 1985. A grim-faced Brezhnev, himself an alcoholic, later featured on a spoof poster that satirised the Soviet anti-alcohol campaign. Alongside portraits of Stalin and Lenin fixed on an office wall, images of Brezhnev and the other leaders frown disapprovingly on two young men who lounge about. Laughing women, with their dresses pulled up to display stocking tops, guzzle champagne as they prance on top of a desk. Several copies of *Pravda* lie in piles on the floor. The poster parodied typical slogans of the Soviet regime, in this case a reminder to young Communists of their duty to work and their duty to the state, but one which became irreverently known to some as the "Work, not Dick" poster.

Brezhnev often seemed unaware about the state of the country, and although the use of vodka as "liquid cash" was forbidden, a story popular at the time neatly summarised how the spirit was still useful as an alternative currency. During a visit to an industrial plant, Brezhnev supposedly asked a machine turner:

> "If I raise the price of a bottle of vodka to ten roubles, will you continue to drink?"
> "Yes."
> "But if I raise the price to twenty roubles?"
> "Yes, Leonid Illyich. You can raise it as high as you like and I shall continue to drink."
> "Why?"
> "Look at this spare part. It costs one bottle of vodka today, and it will always cost one bottle of vodka tomorrow!"

When asked about Russia's vodka problem, Brezhnev replied, "The Russians have always drunk vodka. They can't get by without it." The image of vodka, as well as appearing in anti-vodka posters, was:

> ...omnipresent in every single art form during the Brezhnev period, creating the impression that is and was the Russians' most cherished companion, in joy, love or sorrow. This was of course an incredibly dangerous image, which very few people in Russia attempted to undermine.

Vodka had always been present in art forms throughout Russian history in varying degrees of quality. Impressive art objects included imperial glass vodka flasks and cups with decorative features such as dancing devils as well as vodka cups adorned with the green snake in silver with bejewelled eyes.

After being used to toast six hundred years of historic events, vodka was preparing – or rather being prepared – to make its own dramatic contribution to world history. It would make its mark on an event that was just as powerful and turbulent as the 1917 Russian revolution. Having come to power in March 1985, Gorbachev decided that it was time that Russia really did "get by without vodka", making the Soviet Union's drink problem his number one priority for reform. Two months after becoming general secretary of the Communist Party, he took the strongest steps to combat alcoholism since 1914. It soon became known that Gorbachev, although not an abstainer, drank very little – something that made him suspect to his compatriots inclined to believe an old saying that Russians only trust each other when they are drunk.

If Gorbachev had simply made vodka difficult to buy, it would have been bad enough. It seemed as if the days of Stalin had returned, when anyone with the smell of alcohol was hauled into police stations. When the drunk tanks across the country were full up, thousands of people were driven out into the countryside and dumped. Every night, hordes of so-called drunks were seen walking back to their homes, often in the middle of the winter, in the dark and cold.

The price of vodka increased, and production of the spirit was reduced. It was Gorbachev's intention that the vodka control would encourage factory and agricultural productivity, as innumerable working days were lost through excessive vodka drinking.

It was only part of a complicated economic revival plan, but the cost of lost vodka revenue was thought to be 100 billion roubles. Although vodka coupons were given out allocating two vodka bottles per month, the spirit was in short supply. Vodka shops opened later, attracting three-hour queues in some of the busiest city areas – a dreadful ordeal during the winter. Vodka had never been particularly cheap, and it took seven hours for the average Moscow worker to earn enough to buy one bottle compared to one hour for an average American wage earner.

Those Russians who felt deprived of vodka could only joke about its shortage, and even Gorbachev is supposed to have enjoyed the following joke at his expense. After standing for hours in a vodka-shop queue near Red Square, two men complain about the delay. One says to the other, "I've had enough – I'm going to the Kremlin and I am going to knock Gorbie's head off." When he returned a few minutes later, he was asked what the situation was, and said: "The queues for people wanting to do the same are even longer than this one."

As the first Christmas under Gorbachev approached, the incentive to make illegal vodka had never been greater, and the run on sugar created a national shortage. A cartoon of 1987 showed a drunk at a restaurant table asking for "three hundred glasses of tea – the sugar separately!"

Satiric verse, referring to the price of vodka, which had reached ten roubles, and Gorbachev's nickname of "Minister Lemonade" or "Komrade Kvas", made it clear that the Russian would always obtain vodka come what may:

> Price it high or price it low
> We shall never let it go,
> You tell Misha, Komrade Kvas
> Even ten's ok by us.

For some, ten roubles was too high, and three years later, Russia was awash with *samogon*, which was causing widespread poisoning and thousands of fatalities.

The better-off alcoholics were turning to eau de cologne and causing a shortage by buying it in boxloads. Soon, *eaudecholics* could only drink during licensing hours and were rationed to two bottles per person. Travellers in the Moscow underground remarked that in the morning it "smelled heavenly", and others told the joke about a man who asked for two bottles of aftershave and one bottle of *eau de cologne*. Knowing what it was for, the assistant asked if he would not prefer three bottles of aftershave as this would be cheaper.

"Certainly not!" the man replied. "One of the drinkers is a lady!"

Substitutes for vodka such as perfume were not new, and were eagerly sought and used during the First World War prohibition. Now the last refuge for the desperate, perfume and eau de cologne were well known to the writer of the only modern poetic masterpiece devoted to vodka, *Moscow-Petushki*. Just how much vodka its Russian creator Benedict Erofeev consumed could not be guessed at even by him, but the spirit was inspirational. The only comparable European work is probably Hugh MacDiarmid's *A Drunk Man looks at the Thistle*, which for exuberance, volume of alcohol, comic humour and erudition, Erofeev's effort easily matches.

Erofeev may have been influenced by *Moscow Taverns*, the series of poems written by Esenin in 1922, which celebrated the lives of those who sought consolation from vodka. Like Esenin, Erofeev wanted his poem to have a broad appeal and not be limited to an academic readership.

The interest in the novelistic prose poem of loosely constructed verse is confirmed by the number of translations that have appeared under different titles. *Moscow-Petushki* has also been published as *Moscow to the End of the Line*, *Moscow Stations* and *Moscow Circle*. The Paris edition, *Moscow on Vodka,* while unfaithful to the original title, has a certain apt succinctness. Because the work is in Russian, certain finely-tuned allusions are inevitably lost in translation, but the overall effect remains comic. It also happens to be an incidental guide to vodka brands of the Soviet Union, referring to Bison Grass, Hunter's Vodka and Coriander Vodka as well as the illegal vodka concoctions that alcoholics drank in desperation.

Nothing is quite as it seems, for although the framework of the poem is a train journey that starts in Moscow and ends seventy-eight miles later at Petushki, the physical journey itself may not have taken place.

Between departing and arriving, a character called Benny recounts a series of episodes and escapades from his life, which involve people who are as outlandish and as fantastic as the tales themselves. Benny is trying to travel to Petushki to see his girlfriend and his son, but his need for vodka, sometimes fulfilled but generally not, contributes to the whole uncertainty of what is real and what is imagined. Petushki is a place of idealistic perfection because Benny's loved ones reside there. It is a utopia too perfect to exist, "where original sin… does not burden anyone there", and can therefore never be visited.

The doubt about the journey taking place on a moving train is evident from the start, for Benny intends to see the Kremlin when next visiting Red Square but always somehow misses it. As he is already blind drunk and staggering in Red Square, knowing this simple fact suggests that everything about the rest of the tale is uncertain except Benny's need to be saturated in vodka.

When the vodka shop is closed at night, Benny endures a living hell until it reopens in the morning, and his desperate efforts to find vodka are both pathetic and absurdly comic. He chats to a wide range of travelling companions who all become drunk together. All Benny's money has gone on vodka and a little food, but he knows he can travel for nothing by giving the conductor a swig of vodka instead of the fare. The comedy is learned and frequently alludes to Russian novels and European life, even mentioning British prime minister Harold Wilson and an imaginary visit to London. *Moscow-Petushki* can only go round in circles, typifying the political system, which then seemed unending.

The characters, almost all of whom have been dragged down by alcoholism, are unable to contribute to the productivity of the state and symbolise the blind alley of Communism. The poem is a vivid comment on the sterility and dullness of Soviet life, which for some could only be endured through a perpetual vodka haze.

Like the Benny of the poem, Erofeev was a telephone-cable layer until he was sacked for drinking; he said that the poem was written to amuse those with whom he worked. They deliberately let the cable become rain-soaked and endlessly delayed the completion of the job so that they could instead play poker, talk and drink vodka.

Erofeev was a brilliant intellectual who won a gold medal for his scholastic achievements when he was young. But he was expelled from Moscow University for erratic behaviour. After an early failed marriage, he settled with his second wife, who encouraged his writing. Dying of throat cancer in 1990, Erofeev just lived long enough to see his work gaining critical acclaim.

Moscow-Petushki first attracted attention in the United Kingdom when it appeared in the form of a play in London's West End in 1994. Tom Courtenay took on the leading role and won the Critics Circle Award for Best Actor for his performance.

An indispensable guide to the poem and the scenes it depicts can be found on a YouTube video, which includes a visit to the Stolichnaya distillery. The all-women tasters there are seen taking bites of apples to cleanse their mouths, a necessity after trying Erofeev's *samogon*-cocktail, The Spirit of Geneva. Its recipe includes the following ingredients:

> White Lilac – 50 grams,
> Anti-perspirant for feet – 50 grams,
> Zhigulkev beer – 200 grams
> Varnish – 150 grams.

With the knowledge of a skilled bartender, Erofeev insisted on the use of White Lilac, "for which there is no substitute. Jasmine, Cypress or Lily of the Valley simply won't do."

Unleashing *samogon* and increasing his own unpopularity, Gorbachev's vodka policy proved to be the unwitting means of his own destruction. In response to the widespread discontent, he reversed the measure. Vodka production increased and was sold everywhere, including in toy shops. Die-hard Communists, opposed to Gorbachev's economic liberalism and determined to salvage something out of the wreckage, attempted to remove him in a coup in August 1991. Rescued temporarily by Boris Yeltsin, the man who would become his successor, Gorbachev finally bowed out after both men formally dissolved the Soviet Union in December 1991.

A celebrated vodka drinker, Yeltsin became the first president of the Russian Federation. It seemed almost symbolic that the priest who baptised Yeltsin was drunk on vodka and dropped baby Boris in the font. Tales of the president's heavy drinking became legion. In Berlin, at a ceremony in August 1994 marking the departure of the last Russian troops from Germany, Yeltsin grabbed the baton from the conductor of the Berlin police orchestra and squirmed on the podium as if he were desperate to visit the lavatory. Disorientated during his stay at the White House when visiting President Clinton in 1995, Yeltsin was found outside the building in his underwear, mumbling something about wanting a pizza. Even *The Simpsons* immortalised his drinking, with the highest reading on a breathalyser being called "Boris Yeltsin".

Seen by the West as a clown, Yeltsin rarely allowed vodka to make him appear anything but mellow. For Russia, his economic policy created hyper-inflation, with grim results. Four thousand roubles would have bought a one-room flat when housing was privatised, but by 1993, it could only buy a kilo of frankfurters. Moscow police discovered the corpses of ten pensioners during an average day. They had usually sold their flats in order to make ends meet or just to buy another bottle of vodka.

The Curative Labour Clinics, which had forcibly held chronic alcoholics, closed in July 1992, pushing 11,000 inmates onto the streets. Some celebrated their release with a drink when they were met by friends clutching welcoming bottles of vodka. Others would soon join the heavy drinkers who were homeless and slept in parks, curling up around a bottle of cheap vodka. Cut and bruised from fights and falls, few would survive the severe winters.

Yeltsin resigned in 1999 and died ten years later. As Russian vodka moved into the 21st century, it began to have a new look and was dressed up neatly for the export market, free of the shackles of both the Imperial and Soviet past.

V

Vodka in Poland and Ukraine

Over the course of several centuries, Poland's borders were stretched, shrunk and frequently mauled by Austria, Prussia and Russia. It was sometimes the unwilling host to foreign habits and customs, including food and alcohol. Partly as a result, Poland never regarded vodka as its only national drink as there were other contenders in the form of beer and mead.

The international trade dispute over the claim to being the true home of vodka had revealed that although one of the earliest written records of the word "vodka" occurred in a Polish document of 1405, it did not define what vodka actually was, but it seems to have been used as an antiseptic.

In 1833, Edmund Spencer made a visit to the Caucuses. In an account of his travels through Poland, he listed in the contents, "Of the Poles – Miserable condition of the peasantry – Their addiction to vodka drinking." Travelling through Austrian-controlled Galicia, he noted:

> I could not but admire the fine manly forms and broad shoulders of the peasantry of Galicia… but I do not think, in so small a town, I ever beheld such a scene of intoxication: vodka, the beloved vodka, was everywhere exposed for sale, not only in the houses, but on stands in the streets, and the peasants, having completed their sales, were then quaffing it as freely as if it was beer. It is remarkable that, of every other race, the Slavonic is the most addicted to this degrading vice; whether in Russia, or well-ordered Austria, or Prussia,

> we find the Slavonic part of the population slaves to their inclination for spirituous liquors.

Spencer's observation that vodka was a popular remedy in Poland for every ailment had been made as early as the 16th century when the spirit was used "for washing the chin after showering". This application was known to Nikolai Gogol's main character in *The Nose*. Unable to accept that his nose has vanished from his face, he wonders if he could have drunk his vodka instead of using it as an aftershave.

If the social pleasures and detrimental effects of vodka for the Polish peasantry were much the same as in Russia, its development as an industry in Poland was a rather different affair.

One or two myths about Polish-produced vodka still exist. The first is that the potato is inferior to the grain in terms of the quality of vodka produced after distillation. The second myth to cast out, repeated *ad infinitum*, is that, "King Jan Olbracht of Poland, in 1546 gave the right to distil and sell spirits to every adult citizen." It was an unlikely gift, as he was lacking in spirit himself after dying in 1501.

The potato, often identified with Polish vodka, did not actually feature in vodka production until the early 19th century. It was also used by some Russian distilleries, whether they owned up to it or not. (Small pink potatoes were harvested in Russia on at least one aristocratic estate during the Russian and Polish vodka prohibitions of the First World War.)

Vodka production in Russia and Poland was firmly established by the middle of the 16th century. In Polish Poznan, about 170 miles west from Warsaw, there were forty-nine distilleries, not counting those on landed estates and monasteries. Vodka was so widely available that it was used as a currency by craftsmen for goods outside Poznan. Gdansk took over from Poznan as the main vodka centre when the success of a Dutchman with a liqueur called Der Lachs was copied by others, and by 1772 Gdansk produced more vodka than anywhere else in Poland. The aristocracy could distil vodka on their land, and as with Russia, this meant that the quality was effectively controlled.

But with its sophisticated equipment, it was Poland rather than Russia which led the Slavonic race in early vodka mass production. Vodka was no longer confined to the unsanitary back room of a tavern, and when the Baczewski family built a distillery in Lvov in 1782, it would go on to become the oldest surviving vodka distillery in the world. Quick to implement new technologies, Baczewski was one of the first anywhere in the world to install a system of "double rectification" in 1832, two years after it was invented by an Irishman, Aeneas Coffey.

In this process, the spirit circulated round and back round stacked sealed columns and was condensed by cold water, thereby increasing the alcohol level and discarding impurities in its progress. This was to become the standard method of distilling alcohol with various modifications, and the old "pot still" method of producing a small amount of spirit would only be used for special or more expensive types of vodka.

Baczewski was an innovator in the way the company exported its goods and advertised them; it proved to be as skilful as Smirnov in its advertising and creation of novelty bottles. In fact, the firm used carafes instead of bottles to contain its vodka in order to make the brand instantly recognisable. The first distiller to use daily aeroplanes to transport its products to Paris and elsewhere, Baczewski also had a contract with two Polish trans-Atlantic liners to supply their vodka. Employing an unusual marketing technique to face brand rivalry straight on, the small print on one Baczewski vodka read, "the only vodka of comparable quality is produced by Pierre Smirnoff of Russia". The compliment was reciprocated by Smirnoff, who based his factory in Lvov after the 1917 revolution.

The world's longest surviving brand name in vodka, Wyborowa, is also Polish and based in Poznan. The test criteria of a competition in 1823 for the "most drinkable straight vodka, without added flavour to mask the basic spirit taste", was part of a drive to improve the generally poor quality of vodka. The judges declared that the winning vodka – made from rye and not potato – was "exquisite" or "wyborny" and the hitherto nameless vodka was christened *Wyborowa.* Despite all of the difficulties imposed by war and the rise of Communism, production of Wyborowa has never been interrupted. In 1927 it became the first vodka in the world to register its name internationally.

Because of Poland's relationship with Russia before and after the 1917 revolution, both countries experienced the prohibition of 1914, the monopoly and the restoration of vodka in 1924. Both countries also experienced the same upswing in vodka drinking. In the late 1950s, Poles consumed two and a half times the amount of vodka they had before the Second World War, but, as in Russia, anti-alcohol drives were not particularly successful. In 1958 the price of vodka in both Poland and Russia was increased as a deterrent.

In the previous year, the average Pole had spent twice as much money on the spirit as on bread, thereby making vodka the most expensive item in the family household budget. Vodka was very much a part of family life – an official survey in an elementary school near Warsaw showed that only two out of 1,700 children had never tasted vodka. Hooliganism caused by drunkenness was widespread, and in the first three months of 1957, the militia arrested more than 71,000 adults and 650 juveniles for drunken behaviour.

After months of disagreement on how to combat drunkenness, the Polish government legislated in 1958 to confine alcoholics to institutions and granted the right of an alcoholic's family to collect his wages. That Poland could not confront its own inability to prevent the damaging effects of excess vodka drinking was seen in the advancing of unlikely conspiracy theories. One deputy who farmed grain claimed that: "The Nazi occupation forces had deliberately fostered production of vodka in order to undermine Poland's resistance."

Dark insinuations continue to swirl around the green serpent, with many Russians and Poles still believing to this day that the Communist regimes encouraged heavy drinking to keep an otherwise discontented people happy, or at least docile. The truth will probably never be known, but it was certainly strange that vodka was always available when other consumer goods were in perpetually short supply.

Such a cynical observation would have been appreciated by Stanislaw Ignacy Witkiewicz, a Polish philosopher, painter and writer, who was known as Witkacy. Unfashionably, he encouraged vodka drinking because of its supposedly positive effects on the artistic, if not peasant, mind. In 1932 he published a philosophical account of addictions, *Narkotyki*, which included comments on the way vodka was drunk in Poland and Russia. Witkacy was extremely open regarding his own bouts of vodka drinking, priding himself on never touching it before shaving. A morphine addict to boot, he concluded that alcohol should be completely forbidden to everyone except for artists and writers who would be allowed it for inspiration.

Days after the Second World War broke out, Witkacy committed suicide in Ukraine and was buried. When the Soviet authorities returned his body to Poland in 1988 for reburial in his family grave, he was given a quasi-state funeral. Murmurings persisted that the wrong body had been sent because the authorities had refused to allow the coffin to be opened, and in 1994 the body was exhumed. An X-ray revealed the bones of a woman with a full set of teeth, whereas Witkacy had worn dentures. It was a final joke Witkacy would have approved of, as clowning was an important part of his artistic philosophy.

After Poland and Russia, Ukraine was the next significant source of early vodka production, although some distilleries used molasses instead of wheat, rye or potatoes as the basic ingredient. Perhaps unfairly, the lowest grade of Ukrainian vodka was considered inferior to even the poorest produced by Russia and Poland and was said to be unfit even for the lowest tavern. Chekhov, who rented a house near Yalta, asked for a visitor to bring a bottle of vodka, because he said that the local supply "stinks of the W.C.".

The vodka-producing area of 18th-century Poland is now mostly located in Ukraine, and travellers who complained about the excessive consumption of vodka in Galicia would be insulting the Ukraine of today. The geographical musical chairs continue, for as we saw, Lvov, the area that was formerly a vodka centre in Poland, is now in Ukraine and known as Lviv.

In an effort to control the abuse of alcohol, vodka prices in present-day Ukraine have been increased to make it prohibitively expensive for those living in rural areas. But even if the vodka were cheap, it would not stop the tradition of producing home-made vodka, the forbidden *samogon* or "moonshine", the continuing curse of Russia, Poland and Ukraine.

In 2005 an internet blogger in Ukraine left helpful instructions on how to make vodka according to a method used by his grandmother. Refining the techniques employed in the mass production of vodka, she used an adapted "pot still" process with an old pressure cooker with a sealed lid and added copper pipes. Her *samogon* enabled versatile bartering, as when six grave diggers dug a cousin's grave in return for four bottles, and a labourer scythed a field for one bottle. The strength of the *samogon* was 96 per cent (192 proof in the US), which was considered quite commonplace, but those who drank it were warned to sit down if they had not eaten. (Spirytus, a Polish vodka with the same high proof, has only recently been allowed to be sold in New York.)

Similarly detrimental results from drinking high-proof vodka were experienced by Trotta, the hero of the novel *The Radeztsky March* by Joseph Roth. Arriving in Galicia just before the First World War, Trotta gradually sinks into alcoholism after tasting the very strong local vodka. He realises too late and only too well, as he is told by the well-seasoned local drinkers, that the 90 per cent vodka does not go to the head, but to the legs.

Ukraine is trying to make its own way in the vast global vodka market, and the most famous producer of many fruit-and-herb-flavoured vodka concoctions is Nemiroff. The firm's famous pepper and honey vodka may be quite similar to the favourite vodka of Peter the Great.

Before vodka became standardised in Russia in 1894, the differences in taste between varieties of vodka can only be guessed at, but it is likely that Khlibna Sloza, or "The Tears of Bread", which is now produced in Ukraine, tastes something like the Russian vodka of the past. It emerged victorious in a blind tasting competition in Ukraine, although its packaging, shown afterwards to the tasters, was considered old-fashioned. Based on the 19th century pre-screw bottle top method of sealing a cork with wax and wrapping the bottle in paper, the packaging was previously used by Smirnov and others as the standard method to bottle vodka.

For sheer romance – something rather lacking in the present-day hard sell of vodka – it is difficult to beat the story of the Ukrainian vodka Zorokovich 1917. Founded by Dan Edelstyn from Hackney in London, the Ukraine-based distillery produces a premium vodka.

Not a businessman but a film-maker, Edelstyn discovered an old typescript of a memoir written by his paternal grandmother, Maroussia Zorokovich, who was from Ukraine. Born in 1898 into a rich family, she was a dancer and writer when she fled to Europe after the 1917 revolution with a friend whom she later married. Eventually settling in Belfast, she died there in comparative poverty in 1943.

The mission to find out about his Ukraine Jewish roots began with a visit in 2008 to Edelstyn's ancestral home village of Douboviazovka. He was astonished to discover that his great-grandfather had owned a vodka distillery there. To avoid destruction, it had been moved brick by brick to Siberia, but when Edelstyn visited the factory, it was run-down and unproductive. Despite being just 28 years old at the time, he was viewed by the local workers as a vodka baron, and they promised him their support.

Launched in 2010, and with features of the original Ukrainian recipe, the distinctive vodka is already supplied to Selfridges in London. The label features black swallows on the bottle – a symbol of his grandmother's migration as well as a reference to her dramatic description of the "black wings all over the sky" in her account of the Russian Revolution.

Part 2

Vodka in the West

Lenin's head in ice – Red Square Bar Las Vegas

UK Smirnoff advertisement from the 1960s

I

Smirnoff to Absolut: The Vodka Houses

How two vodka producers became giants and took vodka into the 21st century

Smirnoff and Absolut are so well known in the world of vodka that they need little in the way of introduction.

But what exactly is in these vodkas? Both companies produce a variety of flavoured vodka, but those who drink the neutral brand leader Smirnoff 21 or Absolut vodka would probably be hard-pressed to say what their dominant tastes are when drunk neat. Yet the Anglo-American and Swedish brands are likely to continue leading the market by the sheer familiarity of their names. Shining brightly on the shelves amid the confusion of strange brands and imports, they already seem like old friends.

It was not always so, and both companies had many difficulties introducing vodka to the US. Once Smirnoff was firmly established in America, consumers understood the spirit's qualities. Absolut did not then have to educate America about vodka, but the company was faced with other challenges.

The problems of selling vodka which faced first Smirnoff and then Absolut typify the challenges of advertising any vodka because its salient qualities – tasteless, odourless and flavourless – have to be promoted as positive attributes.

Neither brands are Russian, although Smirnoff makes references to its Russian "origins" dating back to 1848, while Absolut, a young Swedish company founded in 1979, recreated an old brand first produced exactly one hundred years earlier whose name had evolved to Absolut Rent Brännvin, or "Absolutely Pure Vodka".

Smirnoff vodka is now so ubiquitous that it is difficult to believe that it seemed destined for obscurity or oblivion several times after 1917 when it was exiled from Russia. It took off in America as a result of a series of haphazard incidents, but progress towards success could not have been better if planned. In 1933 Vladimir Smirnov sold his company P. A. Smirnoff, which was based in France and tottering towards bankruptcy, to Rudolph Kunett in America. Vodka had never really appealed to the French, who preferred their cognacs and brandies, and the company had become a liability to Vladimir Smirnoff.

The acquisition seemed a wise move on Kunett's part because there had been no opportunity for anyone to introduce any vodka into the United States. The end of prohibition, due in 1933, was the ideal time to launch a new spirit.

Although living in America, Kunett was a Russian émigré whose family had supplied the grain to the Smirnov family before the revolution. Now licensed to use all of the Smirnoff trademarks, bottle shapes, labels and the "exact" Smirnoff recipe, Kunett opened a factory in Connecticut. Unfortunately, it appeared that America had little interest in vodka, and Kunett's enterprise looked as if it would sink before it could ever swim.

The difficulty in selling vodka in America in the 1930s was that the spirit was practically unknown, and a nation grateful for the repeal of the prohibition law drank its old favourites. In a desperate effort to save the company after five years of near failure, Kunett went into partnership in 1939 with John Martin, who ran a pre-mixed drink business called G. F. Heublein & Bros. Martin paid $14,000 for his rights to a share of Smirnoff, and because of the apparent risk, the deal was known as "Martin's folly" by his detractors. But it proved to be a brilliant marriage, which saved Smirnoff.

The rise of Smirnoff in America began through a happy

misdescription. The caps of Heublein's first batches of vodka read "whiskey" because Martin had none that read "vodka". A bright distributor in South Carolina produced an ingenious slogan – "Smirnoff White Whiskey: no taste, no smell!" – to bypass the mislabelling, and a great spirit was born anew.

It was a joy to surreptitious drinkers – "The drink that doctors like because it has no smell" – but when America entered the Second World War and all alcohol production was reduced, Smirnoff was again under threat. The firm needed a sales boost and was given one that was so powerful that the company's finances were secure for the foreseeable future. This dramatic surge in vodka sales was due to the birth of the cocktail, The Moscow Mule.

Several legends surround the circumstances of its creation, thus making it impossible to establish a definitive account. The story that is generally accepted sees Kunett and Martin meeting an old friend, Jack Morgan, in a New York hotel in 1941. Morgan was a Los Angeles ginger beer producer who hoped to market his soft drink in New York. As Morgan remembered: "We three were quaffing a slug [of vodka], nibbling an *hors d'oeuvre* and shoving toward inventive genius."

Kunett and Martin wondered what the result would be if they mixed a two ounce measure of vodka with the ginger beer as well as ice and a touch of lime. Drinking the concoction in a small copper mug, they decided that the experiment was a success, naming the cocktail The Moscow Mule because it had such a kick to it. Morgan promoted the copper mug as an essential element of the drink, and mugs were engraved with its name circling an image of a bucking, grinning mule.

In December 1942 the first mention of the cocktail's success came in "Inside Hollywood", a gossip column by Edith Gynn of *The Hollywood Reporter*:

> There is a new drink that is a craze in the movie colony now. It is called "Moscow Mule". Recipe: equal parts vodka, lime juice and ginger beer!

The recipe was not accurate, as the drink usually contains two parts vodka, one part lime juice and three parts ginger beer. There is no mention of the mug, which did not feature in advertisements until 1945, and the introduction of copper had to wait until 1948 – casting some doubt on the details of the 1941 birth story. The cocktail might in reality have had more prosaic origins as The Moscow Mule had a predecessor with the same ingredients apart from the spirit. Named after an opera singer, the Mamie Taylor was fashionable before prohibition and largely vanished because of it. Made with two measures of whisky, the juice of half a lime, ginger beer to taste and lime for garnish, it would have been a simple step to substitute vodka and adjust the other ingredients to create a vodka cocktail.

Whatever the truth, it is generally agreed that the Moscow Mule kick-started the American fashion for vodka cocktails, but although it became a favourite of Hollywood within a year, its sales only accelerated after the end of the war. A Smirnoff advertisement of 1946 focusing on the Moscow Mule also stressed that vodka could be drunk in soft drinks other than ginger beer in which "it loses itself". Included in the advertisement was the first appearance of the slogan, "It leaves you breathless", which would be used by Smirnoff for thirty-seven years until 1983. The phrase was a clever part of Smirnoff's sales pitch. As the firm would later say, the slogan "alluded to the vodka's virtual lack of an odour, an important component for those consumers who did not want their breath to announce their drinking."

The day after the Korean War began in June 1950, in protest at Soviet support for North Korea, New York bartenders paraded banners saying, "Smirnoff go home. We can do without Moscow Mule". Reported on the front page of *The New York Daily News*, the free publicity encouraged a run on the cocktail and Smirnoff was able to reply to its critics that home was *not* in Russia and that the grain used for its vodka was one hundred per cent American-grown.

After many different types of sales campaigns, which varied from country to country where the licensing franchise was held, there was no unified message explaining what Smirnoff vodka was all about. Hublein had sold out to International Distillers and Vintners (IDV) in 1987, but it took another six years before the US-based company drastically changed its entire policy on advertising.

Smirnoff had been the market leader of vodka but found that its sales were deteriorating. Russian brands such as Stolichnaya had a slight impact on Smirnoff's sales, but the Swedish upstart Absolut had invaded America in 1979, and as its sales increased, Smirnoff's declined. Smirnoff was told that it needed to reinvent itself to attract a new, younger age group of 18–24 year olds. The vodka recipe would of course remain unchanged, for it was important not to alienate loyal customers. Its selling points – purity combined with a lack of smell, colour and taste – were maintained. It was most usefully a chameleon drink – adaptable, versatile and ostensibly innocent. At the same time, it had a daringly "mischievous" image.

These characteristics were summed up in a new slogan, "pure thrill". It was a phrase that could be adapted according to its context, and it was launched in December 1995 in an award-winning series of UK television advertisements entitled "Message through a bottle". (TV advertisements for alcoholic products were still banned in the US.) The adverts promoted the idea that life seen through a bottle of Smirnoff was more exciting than what went on outside of it.

One advertisement featuring a bottle of Smirnoff being passed round at a wedding reception showed the bride as a vampire about to bite into her new husband. The phrase "pure thrill" became "pure surprise" when a pair of ice tongs were revealed as an oyster with a pearl. The campaign was a brilliant success for IDV, with Smirnoff vodka besting Bacardi Rum as the global market leader for all spirits.

After many years of advertising the contents of the Smirnoff bottles as opposed to their shape, Smirnoff's new parent company Diageo decided that a fresh bottle design was overdue. A new look, with labels depicting a "regal eagle", was described as "the new elegant brand icon". It hinted at Smirnoff's Russian past and was launched in July 2010.

Absolut vodka was launched in the US in 1979 and sold 12,000 cases. By 1991 it was selling 2.7 million cases a year. It was a success story that the Swedish government, which made the supply of alcohol a state monopoly, could not have anticipated even when it first considered that vodka could be a valuable export. Any new vodka had to succeed in America, and the Swedish government was prepared to invest large sums of money to make sure that it did. Sweden was well aware of Smirnoff's market domination in the US, and it was important that any Swedish product would have to be as unlike Smirnoff in every way except quality.

It would also have to trump other vodka brands competing in America since Smirnoff's arrival, including Finnish Finlandia and Stolichnaya, a favourite of Freddie Mercury, from Russia. Stolichnaya, billing itself as "the only genuine Russian vodka", had been exclusively imported by Pepsi since 1974 in exchange for cola syrup in Russia, but whenever there was a political incident between Russia and the United States, the Americans refused to handle the incoming cargo. Supplies on shop shelves were unreliable, while Finlandia made little impact on the market and, like Stolichnaya, posed no real threat.

Absolut state that their vodka was derived from a brand produced in 1879 by Lars Olsson Smith. In his day, Olsson Smith was known as the "king of vodka", and an image of his face featured on the bottle alongside the words: "Vodka has been sold under the name Absolut since 1879." Other sources suggest that Absolut was created from a new recipe. Börje Karlsson, the master blender for the Swedish government, decided that the vodka should taste like a cross between Smirnoff and a Finnish vodka, Koskenkorva. The Finnish vodka was so pure that it was almost tasteless, while Smirnoff had character because some impurities were deliberately left in.

The company also analysed every known brand of vodka, comparing the results with its own experiments. Although all of the impurities were scientifically extracted and listed, Karlsson relied on his nose as the final judge of what was to be left in. The decisive factor was a whiff of freshly baked bread, redolent of wheat grain – a feature that characterized many Imperial Russian vodkas. Karlsson had already discovered that mixing a Bloody Mary did not disguise a bad-tasting element of a vodka, but instead accentuated it. The new vodka had to pass the tomato juice test as well.

What would become Absolut seemed almost ready for production when the prospective American importer arrived and stated that no vodka in America would sell unless it passed the "ice test". When a bottle of freezer-stored Stolichnaya was poured, the liquid slipped out slowly like thick oil, and any new vodka would have to emulate this or it would not be accepted as true vodka. Stolichnaya was a genuine Russian vodka and was not stored in the freezer in Russia. But in America its qualities were altered by freezing and this was judged to be the prototype of what America considered acceptable as representing a vodka taste.

It is widely agreed in Russia that vodka should not be stored in the freezer because the extreme temperatures start to undo the distillation process and destroy the natural wheat bouquet of Russian vodka. Russian Standard, for example, suggests that the ideal temperature for chilled vodka is between 4–5 degrees Celsius or 41–44 Fahrenheit.

The vodka had been deliberately stripped of some Russian characteristics, but impurities such as fusel oil, which had been removed, were returned by degrees until the potential Absolut importer felt that the icy flow was slow enough. The formula for Absolut had been created and the vodka was ready to be bottled.

The design of the bottle was as important as the contents. The Smirnoff "pure thrill" slogan lay in the future, but Absolut decided that the purity of its vodka would be seen as part of its image along with the bottle itself. When it was advertised, the image of Absolut would not be cluttered with unnecessary verbiage, but reduced to two words whenever possible, one of which would always be Absolut.

The emphasis that the Absolut design team placed on the bottle shape, the lettering and the size of the cap was the subject of heated internal wrangling, as trial shapes were considered and rejected. The vodka bottle had to leave no doubt as to its contents and to be noticed on shop shelves, but it could not resemble the shape of the traditional vodka bottles such as Smirnoff. There would be no paper label to obscure the transparency of the vodka or the container, and therefore everything that did appear on the bottle had to count.

The bottle eventually selected was based on an old Swedish medicine container that was found in an antique shop. Silver lettering was rejected in favour of the blue that is still used. The look of the bottle worked despite the fact that some bartenders complained that the clear bottle meant customers would not see that it was there. They also said that its squat shape made it hard to pick up quickly.

Absolut trumpeted the originality of the bottle design by commissioning a series of adverts by artists, which paired their names with the brand's. "Absolut Warhol" launched the series in 1985, and the company combined its efforts with Damien Hirst in 1998. The artist-designed bottles were by that time completely identified with the product.

An early advertisement in America was called "Absolut Heaven" and saw the bottle sprouting angel wings. Placed in the *New York Times* at a budget rate, which gave no guarantee of when or where the advertisement would appear in the newspaper, it featured by chance opposite the obituaries.

The Absolut series of advertisements is said to be the longest ongoing series in advertising history and developed into a unique phenomenon, which saw the company commission over 300 painters as well as sculptors, glass designers, musicians and fashion designers. Absolut even stepped across the East-West vodka border and commissioned twenty-six Russian artists to create their own versions of the bottle to celebrate *glasnost*.

Absolut attracted some critical comments due to a series of adverts for the blackcurrent-flavoured Absolut Kurant, which were literally laced with sexual innuendo with their inclusion of easily undone black leather corsets. Hinting at sex and kinkiness was never going to harm the company, but it did take more of a brand risk in the pre-Internet era by being amongst the first large retail companies to place adverts in American, and later European, non-pornographic gay magazines. Absolut produced those adverts as early as 1981 and went on to sponsor many gay events, as it still does.

An explicitly gay advertisement called "Ruler Absolut" took what the company called at the time "a humorous look at gay men and their fascination for the perfect, eight-inch 'member' measurements". But although Absolut declared itself to be the "preferred brand of vodka for gay and lesbian consumers", it was not the only vodka that targeted the gay market. Other rivals included Finlandia with its "Naked Finn, straight up, but never straight" adverts as well as SKYY and Svedka. The latter ran three separate adverts: "Gay men still prefer Svedka over sex with women"; "Gay women still prefer Svedka over sex with men"; and, to be completely politically correct, "I Go Both Ways".

Missing the gay target with limp-wristed efforts were a few Smirnoff contributions. One included a rainbow-coloured scarf wound round a vodka bottle and a slogan which could have been aimed at any vodka consumer group. Nevertheless, Smirnoff had promoted an advertisement aimed at the gay market as early as 1958. The advert depicts two men in grey clothing with one seated at a table along with a bottle of Smirnoff and a couple of glasses. The other dandified man stands close behind him, adopting a wilting pose as he puts his hand on his companion's back. The caption reads, "Mixed or straight – it leaves you breathless."

Absolut was so familiar to Americans by 2004 that it was the brand chosen by the character Samantha in the US TV series *Sex and the City* to promote the flagging career of her boyfriend, Smith Jared, played by Jason Lewis. Featuring a fictitious Absolut advertisement captioned "Absolut Hunk", it showed Lewis naked apart from a carefully placed bottle of vodka and was posted on billboards in New York. In the story, the publicity was such a success that a cocktail named Absolut Hunk was created and guzzled by the main characters. When the programme was broadcast, Absolut obligingly issued a press release including the recipe for a quickly-invented Absolut Hunk cocktail, and Manhattan bars were swamped with requests for it.

But although Absolut and Smirnoff benefited enormously from

such exposure, both brands suffered the occasional advertising-related setback as they pushed the boundaries of taste in their hunt for attention. Absolut erred in 2008 with a Mexican advertising campaign, which led to a storm of protest in the US at the depiction of a "perfect world" in which Texas was still a part of Mexico. Following a barrage of complaints from survivors of the Titanic disaster, Smirnoff withdrew an advert featuring a vodka-sipping shipwrecked passenger of the Titanic clutching a lifebelt and declaring, "Well, they said anything could happen". Part of an iconic series of advertisements launched by Smirnoff in the 1970s, it was the only one that attracted objections.

Dating back to the 1970s, the series of "before and after" situations included one advert with the caption, "I was the mainstay of the Public Library until I discovered Smirnoff". It features a previously ardent library user, who has been transformed into a buxom woman with laced boots, sitting on a chair in a forest while a closed book lies on top of a chest. No vodka glass or bottle is present, but the Smirnoff logo is surmounted by the slogan of the advertising series, "The effect is shattering".

The challenge of creating the advertisements was given by the then owners of Smirnoff, International Distillers & Vintners, to the advertising agency Young & Rubicam. The art director David Tree struggled with his copywriter John Bacon to find an imaginative presentation, which had to avoid the spirit's Russian origins because of the association with firewater. Tree noticed a magazine pin-up on the office wall and remarked to Bacon that if they were stuck they could always say, "I was a boring housewife in Southgate until…", referring to the area of north London where he lived. The genesis of the campaign was as simple as that.

The advertisements, which mocked the middle-class habits of the middle-aged vodka consumer, were considered progressive and slightly daring in the 1970s, now look dated compared to the techniques employed by today's vodka goliaths.

But if Smirnoff ever lagged behind Absolut in marketing technique, it had one weapon Absolut would never have: the power of 007 and James Bond. Fortunately for Smirnoff, Bond would order nineteen vodka martinis in Ian Fleming's novels and short stories.

Sean Connery as James Bond

II

Vodka in the UK and the USA

W. & A. Gilbey, a British company famous as a gin distiller, announced in its annual report for 1954 that it:

> began to market a British vodka during the year, feeling that, in view of the vogue for vodka which has swept the USA, there would be a demand for the "all purposes spirit" in this country. We were fortunate in persuading the present owners of the recipe for "Smirnoff – the greatest name in vodka"– to allow us to make it under licence and we have been well pleased with the results to date.

"Well pleased" now seems like an old-fashioned and understated phrase to use about a product that would become the number one choice of spirits in the UK, but neither Gilbey, the first company to manufacture vodka in England, nor anyone else could have anticipated just how great the vodka vogue would become. The following year, after boosting the vodka's strength, Gilbey's annual report stated that their vodka sales were still slow even as they increased with every month. There was little historical appetite for the spirit, with demand confined to East End London pubs in Russian-Jewish immigrant areas, which had been stocking vodka for half a century.

It took some time for vodka even to be noticed, and it was not Smirnoff but Polish vodka that was advertised most frequently. With a distinctly un-British disregard for propriety, it boasted of having the "highest alcohol" content in the world. Its instruction to drink the vodka and not to "bother about meals at all" made it sound intent on corrupting the perfect housewife and leading her into a life of domestic idleness:

> HERE'S PROOF 140% – The highest alcohol content in the world is now on sale in Britain! Here's something to set those cocktails wagging, make you the life of the party, make it the party of your life. Take it any way you like – strong (Pure Spirit) or mild (Bison Brand), straight (Vyborova) or styled (Cherry Vodka) – take it before meals, after meals, with meals, or why bother about meals at all? It's actually distilled and bottled in Poland. Ask for Polish vodka!

Two years later, Smirnoff advertised vodka as a cooling summer drink: "The genial mixer – *21* is wondrously, breathlessly smooth… if you like it with gin, you'll love it with Smirnoff." By then, sales of vodka in Britain had exceeded all expectations, rocketing between 1959 and 1961. In seven years, vodka sales increased by 15,000 per cent, but the spirit was not considered particularly significant by the British Parliament.

A bill that was to adjust the volume of spirits served in public houses and elsewhere was debated in the House of Commons, but when it reached the House of Lords, it was noticed that vodka had been left out. The bill stated that, "gin, rum, and whisky drunk on licensed premises should be sold only in measures of one quarter, one fifth, or one sixth of a gill, or multiples of these amounts."

The Duke of Atholl asked that vodka should be included, because vodka distributors believed that the spirit would be given a bad name if it was thought that it was being sold in short measure. The government had left vodka out because it considered its sales to be negligible. But the duke replied that the 100,000 proof gallons drunk in 1960 represented a 100 per cent increase on 1959. He noted that consumption of vodka in the US as recently as 1948 was "virtually nil", but that twelve years later, eleven million gallons of vodka were drunk there every year.

He did his own research in various bars in London's West End, "at great cost both to my pocket and no doubt eventually to my health", and discovered that in the winter, vodka and rum sales were more or less the same. But in the summer, vodka sales were anything from three to six times those of rum. Publicans had told him that vodka sales were "increasing fairly fast and fairly substantially".

Lord Shackleton noted Scotland's very high alcohol consumption and remarked that it had increased there by 150 per cent. He added that, according to favourable publicity, "you could drink vodka without becoming fat, spotty, or developing a hangover". He concluded that vodka was, "obviously likely to be the sort of drink which will rank, perhaps on a lesser stage, alongside gin and whisky and rum." It was agreed that vodka should be included with the other spirits because the bill would not become law for another three years, and it was supposed that by then, the anticipated increase in vodka sales would justify its inclusion.

The question as to why vodka had become so popular in such a short period of time was asked as early as 1962. While it was clear that vodka was essentially a young person's drink, exactly why this was the case has still not been explained. It was suggested at the time that the spirit had a certain glamour, which inclusion within the Bond films of 1962 and 1963 served to further. Even the space age was thought by *The Times* to have made a contribution to its success, but it warned readers that vodka was "a rough, fiery spirit likely to lead the drinker into unspeakable excesses". It noted that, "contrary to popular belief, most of the vodka sold in this country is distilled here ...There are nearly a dozen producers in this country."

These British firms had the potential to exploit the increase in vodka drinking, but apart from Gilbey, few of them seemed to realise the market possibilities and consequently did not advertise. Wolfschmidt only promoted a liqueur, although its vodka was favoured by "M" in the Bond novels and was the only brand of vodka named by Ian Fleming in his fiction.

By the time vodka in Europe and America became the most popular spirit, it was respectable and socially acceptable, and there was little about the spirit that was "rough or fiery", a more apposite description when referring to some Russian vodkas when drunk neat. All of the promotions of vodka in the 1960s were as part of a drink in which tomato juice, vermouth, orange or lime could be added. It was the era of the vodka cocktail in Britain, the most famous of which was the Bloody Mary. Already popular for some years in America, its origins are enshrined in myth both as to when it was invented and the woman behind the name. Who is Mary? Nobody really knows.

The New York Herald Tribune of 1939 noted that "George Jessel's newest pick-me-up, which is receiving attention from the town's paragraphers, is called a Bloody Mary: half tomato juice, half vodka." Jessel was an actor, and it is likely that his contribution was the vodka and tomato juice but not all of the ingredients, which according to the *Oxford English Dictionary* should include: "vodka, tomato juice, and other (usually pungent) flavourings, typically served with a celery stalk or similar garnish."

No doubt glad to earn a fee from Smirnoff, Jessel appeared in an advertisement, declaring with a slight hesitation that:

> "I, GEORGE JESSEL, INVENTED THE BLOODY MARY"
> "I *think* I invented the Bloody Mary, Red Snapper, Tomato Pickup or Morning Glory" reports George Jessel. "It happened on a Night before a Day, and I felt I should take some good, nourishing tomato juice, but what I really wanted was some of your good Smirnoff vodka. So I mixed them together, the juice for body and the vodka for spirit, and if I wasn't the first ever, I was the happiest ever."

The spicy flavour, which has made the cocktail famous, was probably concocted by Fernand Petiot, a barman from Harry's Bar in Paris, who later worked in the Hotel St. Regis in New York. He told a feature writer that he had initiated the:

> Bloody Mary of today. George Jessel said he created it, but it was really nothing but vodka and tomato juice when I took it over. I cover the bottom of the shaker with four large dashes of salt, two dashes of black pepper, two dashes of cayenne pepper, and a layer of Worcestershire Sauce; I then add a dash of lemon juice and some cracked ice, put in two ounces of vodka and two ounces of thick tomato juice, shake, strain, and pour.

He also claimed that one of the first customers he made the drink for came from Chicago where there was a bar called Bucket of Blood and a waitress whom everybody called “Bloody Mary”. The customer said that the drink reminded him of her, “and the name stuck”.

Yet another version of the cocktail’s birth, which seems the most likely, was promoted in 2009 by the St. Regis Hotel when it announced a series of celebrations for the 75th birthday of the Bloody Mary. In this version of events, the drink was conceived five years earlier in 1934, with Petiot creating it for Prince Serge Obolensky, a rich Russian émigré who asked for a vodka cocktail similar to one he had enjoyed in Paris.

The Bloody Mary was one of the few concoctions that survived when cocktails went out of fashion and habits changed. By the 1970s, younger drinkers of all classes were socialising in public houses, and the more formal party, where the cocktail dress was once *de rigeur*, became an increasingly rare event. For many young drinkers in the mid-1990s, their first introduction to vodka, and indeed alcohol, came by way of a vodka cocktail in the form of alcopops, but the latter were very distant cousins of the classic cocktail. The ready-prepared combinations of alcohol and a coloured mixer of fruit or lemonade were condemned by the Church and others, for being carefully created in alluring colours to “seduce young people into the evils of drinking”.

The more vivid colours of alcopops make them anything but macho. The luridly coloured blue and red bottles of WKD and a range of Smirnoff Ice products appeal primarily to young women. Both companies were ordered to remove their UK television adverts by the Advertising Standards Authority in 2006. The ASA objected to WKD's use of "juvenile" humour, which would appeal to young people, and the Smirnoff Ice advert's characters Uri and Gorb were adjudged "likely to become cult figures with strong appeal to under-18s".

Moscow Mule Mug

III

James Bond and Films

It has often been said that James Bond's vodka martini revolutionised the cocktail in America and finished off the gin martini. But Smirnoff's Moscow Mule first opened up the possibilities of using vodka instead of gin in cocktails and predates the vodka martini, which appears for the first time in Ian Fleming's second Bond novel, *Live and Let Die*, published in 1954.

Nevertheless, the importance of vodka in its association with James Bond and the phrase "shaken, not stirred" cannot be underestimated, especially as alcohol could not be advertised on American television.

In Fleming's first 007 novel, *Casino Royale*, published in 1953, Bond orders a dry martini made with both vodka and gin, and details the recipe to the barman. The same recipe appears in an identical form in the most recent film adaptation of the novel starring Daniel Craig. He names the cocktail The Vesper after the main love interest in the film, and it is also drunk by Bond in the 2008 film *Quantum of Solace*. The ingredients of the drink have since had to be modified, as the vermouth Kina Lillet no longer exists except in a reincarnated version called Lillet Blanc, which had some of the quinine removed to make it less bitter. To match the strength of the Gordon's gin, Gordon's Export, rather than their standard gin, must now be used.

Gin was banished from the vodka martini, which made its debut in the novel *Live And Let Die* in 1954. Bond tells Solitaire how to mix it but not with the "shaken and not stirred" phrase, which is not mentioned anywhere until *Dr. No*.

From then on, the vodka martini occurred more often in the films than in the books. Bond does not restrict his enjoyment of vodka to the martini he made famous. The secret agent enjoys a plain vodka and tonic in Istanbul in *From Russia With Love*, in which the vodka is passable, albeit flooded with tonic. The same drink is enjoyed in *On Her Majesty's Secret Service* and *Thunderball* along with a dash of Angostura bitters. When with M in *Moonraker*, 007 drops a pinch of pepper into his vodka to sink the fusel oil to the bottom whilst carefully removing with his finger a few remaining specks of pepper that remain on the top. As M drinks Wolfschmidt, a perfectly pure vodka, the pepper refinement really betrays how little Bond knows about vodka brands.

Earlier in the day, before he has dinner with Goldfinger in England, Bond has several vodka and tonics, and endures a lecture that evening by his host. Goldfinger expiates on the evils of both smoking and drinking, including the poison of fusel oil in alcohol. Bond shows off his knowledge of vodka distillation, explaining that he drinks the spirit because he has heard that:

> "…its filtration through activated charcoal is a help."
> Bond, dredging this piece of expertise out of dim recollections of something he had read, was rather proud of having been able to return Goldfinger's powerful serve.
> Goldfinger glanced at him sharply. "You seem to understand something of these matters. Have you studied chemistry?"
> "Only dabbled in it." It was time to move on…

The "shaken, not stirred" line recurred in many of the Bond films and was parodied elsewhere. Bugs Bunny delights in a carrot martini, which emerges from a car dashboard at the push of a button, and is announced by the car with, "Shaken, not stirred, sir?" The first novel to use the phrase in the narrative was *Diamonds Are Forever* (1956), but it was first uttered in *Dr. No* by Julius No. Bond himself began using the immortal phrase in *Goldfinger*.

Does shaking rather than stirring make any difference at all to the taste of the cocktail? The question was considered in a rather tongue-in-cheek scientific analysis carried out in Canada:

> *Shaken, not stirred:* bioanalytical study of the antioxidant activities of martinis.
>
> *Background*: Moderate consumption of alcoholic drinks seems to reduce the risks of developing cardiovascular disease, stroke, and cataracts, perhaps through antioxidant actions of their alcohol, flavonoid, or polyphenol contents.
>
> "Shaken, not stirred," routinely identifies the way the famous secret agent James Bond requires his martinis.
>
> *Objectives*: As Mr Bond is not afflicted by cataracts or cardiovascular disease, an investigation was conducted to determine whether the mode of preparing martinis has an influence on their antioxidant capacity.

After detailing several pages of the laboratory analysis, the scientists noted that, "Shaken martinis were more effective in deactivating hydrogen peroxide than the stirred variety." It also concluded that:

> Although the reason for the superior antioxidant activity of shaken martinis is not clear, is it possible that James Bond chose shaken martinis because of the improved antioxidant potential? This added antioxidant effect could result, of course, in a healthier beverage.
>
> Conclusion: 007's profound state of health may be due, at least in part, to compliant bartenders.

Almost the last word on the subject came from correspondence in *New Scientist* magazine in which it was suggested that when Fleming was writing, the vodka that he drank was probably made from potato rather than grain. Indeed, in *Dr. No*, Bond asks that the vodka should be Polish, not Russian. That Fleming might have been partial to Polish potato-based vodkas could explain the origins of the "shaken, not stirred" line, because vodka made from potato can have an oily taste – often described as creamy – and this can be reduced when shaken with ice. In an experiment with potato- and grain-based vodkas, a reader of the *New Scientist* assembled a group of vodka-drinking guinea pigs:

> First we tasted the vodkas. In the blind trial, all six people in our sample said the potato vodka was oily and the grain vodka wasn't. Then we made two vodka martinis using the potato vodka. One was stirred with ice, the other shaken with ice. The difference was quite distinct and in a blind tasting every one of the six drinkers characterised the shaken martini as being much less oily. But the martini had to be consumed quickly. If left to settle for five minutes or so, the shaken martini became oily again.

It is a conceivable explanation for the phrase's gestation, but despite these conjectures, it seems more likely that Fleming would himself drink M's favoured Wolfschmidt, which is made from grain.

Although Smirnoff is used in the films, Bond's favourite vodka was the Russian Stolichnaya, which he drinks in *Licence to Kill*, when it is doctored with chloral hydrate. He also drinks it from the bottle in Sebastian Faulks' Fleming-Bond pastiche, *Devil May Care*.

The frequent mention of vodka in the Bond novels made the film versions ideal means for product placement. It was a massive boon for Smirnoff given that alcoholic product advertisements have been limited to cable television in America, and only since 1996. As the most famous vodka in America and Europe, Smirnoff was the obvious choice for featuring in the Bond films. It appeared in the first film, *Dr. No*, and is clearly visible in a long, hovering camera shot over the bottle in a hotel in *Tomorrow Never Dies*. It also features in *The World is not Enough*.

The famous Smirnoff-Bond association lasted for nearly 40 years, but when MGM were planning *Die Another Day* with Pierce Brosnan as Bond, Smirnoff did not take up their usual product placement option. It was probably the result of the attempt beginning in 1995 to modernise the company's image. Smirnoff stated that they were really trying to attract consumers who were "more in the 21 to 29 age group. People in that age group socialise more… and that fits in with their perceptions of Smirnoff and when it's best enjoyed. Bond's audience is men aged 25 to 45. James Bond isn't about socialising with friends. Bond is about status and being cool."

MGM retorted that the Bond target audience included men and women between the ages of thirteen and fifty-nine, but an American research group suggested that Bond enthusiasts were disproportionately located at each end of the age scale. Teenage boys liked Bond because of video game spin-offs, and men over thirty-five were often Bond devotees. In both cases, vodka promotions were inadvisable as the boys were too young, while members of the older group tended to be less promiscuous in their drinking habits and were already wedded to their favourite vodka.

Finlandia was delighted to accept the product placement. Its global marketing director for sales crowed, "this is an unbelievable coup for us", before adding that, "Finlandia's image fits perfectly with the film's ice theme. Finlandia's image is cold, clean, natural and icy. Our bottle is patterned after glacial ice."

With a slight dig at Smirnoff, a spokeswoman added that "the typical Finlandia drinker is aged between twenty-five and thirty-nine, when customers have more discretionary income and are developing a taste for higher-quality vodka." The deal with MGM was reported to have cost Finlandia $1 million. When the film appeared, the product's name was never spoken. Instead, Pierce Brosnan ventures to Iceland, where a bar is carved into the interior of an ice palace, and its icy shelves are stacked with bottles of Finlandia.

The fling between Bond and Finlandia ended when *Casino Royal* was produced in 2006 and featured Smirnoff stands in a couple of scenes. Although it ran a Bond-related advert when the film came out, Smirnoff's product placement in *Casino Royale* was positively demure by the standards of the franchise. Smirnoff returned almost as an afterthought to support the secret agent in *Quantum of Solace*, with a special limited edition of Smirnoff *Quantum of Solace* Black Vodka. By the time of the film franchise's 50th anniversary and the release of *Skyfall* (2012), vodka's association with Bond was blown out of the water by a rumoured $45 million tie-up with Heineken.

Vodka cocktails in films and on TV have not always been taken so seriously, especially those concocted by Homer Simpson. In the 2010 season of *The Simpsons*, he shakes up a large measure of vodka in a mayonnaise jar and after drinking it, collapses immediately. He has however invented a cocktail redolent of wheatgrass called The Lawnmower, which he shares with a neighbour in an episode made in 1989.

Less frivolously, vodka was a constant feature in the film based on the novel *Hot Snow*, which centres on the Battle of Stalingrad. It is memorably drunk from tins into which newly-awarded war medals have been dropped. A vehicle for comedy in *The Irony of Fate*, vodka almost headed the *dramatis personae* in the film, which was shown in Russia on almost every New Year's Eve after it was released in 1976. It revolves around the character of Zhenya, a vodka lover who gets drunk and accidentally flies to Leningrad from Moscow to celebrate the New Year. It is as popular in Russia as *It's a Wonderful Life*. The annual showing of the film ceased during the Gorbachev period, when it and other films appearing to glorify vodka were banned, but a sequel has since been produced, which features the children of the original characters.

The relatively late appearance of vodka in America meant that it did not feature in films until the 1930s, when the world's most famous butler took part in the Hollywood comedy *Step Lively, Jeeves!* (1937). The P. G. Wodehouse character goes to America to claim a fortune only to find that he has been duped by a fake Russian prince, who plies him with vodka until he is drunk. The spirit is described as "the nectar of cherubs and angels", and the film, using vodka to "authenticate" the scene, is a reflection of how the spirit was still considered in America to be a Russian drink.

Vodka has had no shortage of starring roles in films set in the Baltic region. In *Take Care of Your Scarf, Tatiana* (1994), two gloomy Finns, Valto and Reino, go wandering in search of coffee and vodka, without which their lives are meaningless. They meet two women, Russian Klaudia and Estonian Tatiana, who want to become more than friends with the men.

The harshness of life, only cheered up by vodka, is a constant theme of two cinematic gems: *The Vodka Factory* and *Vodka Lemon*. The award-winning, Swedish-produced film *The Vodka Factory* is beautifully filmed, from the opening shots of vodka bottles being packed from a conveyor belt to atmospheric snowscapes. A fictional story shot in the style of a documentary, it focuses on Valya, a 22-year-old single mother who works in a local vodka factory. She lives with her son and her mother in a backwoods Russian town where there is nothing to do but drink vodka. Valya would have to leave her son behind to fulfil her dreams of becoming an actress in Moscow. It seems she can only create fantasies of a world she can never have.

Filmed in Armenia and directed by Hiner Saleem, *Vodka Lemon* is an outstanding film, which, set against a background of never melting snow, is characterised by warm humour that frequently borders on the absurd. In an Armenian village financially ruined by the Soviet collapse, Hamo (Romen Avinian), a Kurdish widower with three useless sons, visits his wife's grave every day, where he meets the widow Nina (Lala Sarkissian). She works in a bar, Vodka Lemon, which is about to close down, and although the couple have scarcely a penny between them, poverty does not hinder the blossoming of a love affair. The production won the Best Film Award at the 2003 Venice Film Festival.

There was no doubt that vodka had arrived in Britain when it featured heavily in the television series *Absolutely Fabulous.* First broadcast in 1992, more than thirty episodes would see vodka, or a vodka cocktail, being an integral part of the life of the bohemians of the London fashion scene.

It has been suggested that when the cocktail was in eclipse, this was due to an increase in the use of recreational drugs, an issue which did not affect the main characters in the series who enjoyed both. The favourite drink of Patsy and Edina, played by Joanna Lumley and Jennifer Saunders respectively, was their own invention of Stoli-Boly, which was made from Stolichnaya vodka and Bollinger champagne. This inspired the creation of the cocktail Absolutely Fabulous in 1999 at Monte's Club in London. A new series was shown in 2011 along with an Olympics special in 2012, about which Joanna Lumley remarked: "The great thing is that… we fast-forwarded to where they're very old and nearly dead and practically plugged into vodka machines."

For vodka excess, it is hard to beat *The Adventures of Priscilla Queen of the Desert*, a cult film of the 1990s about a group of drag queens swilling vodka while crossing the Australian desert in a bus called Priscilla. Terence Stamp plays Bernadette Basinger, a transvestite who is challenged in an outback country bar to a drinking contest by a fat, vulgar Australian woman. They drink *Stolichnaya* vodka and when the abusive woman loses to the drag queen, Basinger gains the admiration of the uncouth locals.

When the film was reincarnated as the Broadway and London musical *Priscilla Queen of the Desert*, it became an ideal means of showcasing particular vodka brands which sponsored, or were associated with, the productions including Grey Goose, Rokk, and Russian Standard.

IV

Vodka Today

Following the collapse of the Soviet Union and the creation of the Russian Federation, there was a vodka free-for-all when Yeltsin abolished the state vodka monopoly. There was no tax on vodka and it was so cheap that it was often used as a cleaner. Russia was flooded with imported vodka, which for a time sold more than domestic brands. Legal battles commenced, with private enterprise trying to register names that had been controlled by the Soviet Union until the Federation managed to stake its claim as the rightful inheritor.

The demolition of the Berlin Wall in 1989 seemed to open up the Russian market to Smirnoff. The Soviet army remained in East Germany for three years but was paid for by West Germany. Previously unavailable western products such as Malborough cigarettes and jeans were bought by the army, which also consumed two hundred bottles of Smirnoff vodka a day. It is easy to forget that the world's most famous vodka was unknown in Russia and the former East Germany, and to meet the demand, twenty thousand bottles a day were flown to Germany from Britain.

It seemed a suitable time to bring Smirnoff into Russia, and a bottle was created with Russian labels and advertising that emphasised the origins of the company. The success in Germany was not repeated in Russia, as the novelty of drinking imported vodka in Russia did not last, and Russians continued to buy familiar, domestic brands.

The arrival of Smirnoff in Russia did not please Boris Smirnov, a former KGB officer and descendant of Pyotr Arsenijevic Smirnov, who had begun to produce vodka from the original recipe that had been preserved in the family. Starting up in the south of Russia with the help of his uncle, Boris eventually leased the original Moscow Smirnov headquarters which had become a garage, furnishing it with 19th-century antiques and decorating the walls with old Smirnov advertisements.

Boris learned of a dispute in 1980 when a Russian-East German spirit exporter sued Smirnoff for trying to import the famous brand. The Russian-German company argued that the Smirnoff label – brandishing the tsarist warrants and the Imperial Eagle, and partly lettered in Cyrillic – misled customers about where it was made. The court was told that the Smirnoff company never had the legal rights to the Smirnoff package of copyrights, recipes and trademarks sold to them by Vladimir Smirnoff in 1933 because he had already disposed of his interests in the Russian Smirnov company in 1905 to his brother Pyotr. The case was settled in an amicable manner, with Smirnoff agreeing to remove the distinctive Russian features from the label and to state clearly that the vodka was not made in Russia.

The result encouraged Boris Smirnov to think that money might be made out of Smirnoff's owners, Diageo, and he sued them using the same arguments that had been raised by the exporter in 1980. The truth of the exact origins of the Russian Smirnov company had been distorted into a myth, he claimed, adding that some of the publicity used by Smirnoff was an invention. Diageo explained that they had bought the company in good faith, and quite apart from the fact that it was almost impossible to prove whether Vladimir had been entitled to sell the company, subsequent owners had prevented Smirnoff from becoming extinct. The Russian Smirnovs felt that Boris was dragging the family name into the mud, and his uncle dissolved their partnership by selling his stake in the company.

On 9 November 2000, armed riot police wearing black masks stormed the Smirnov Moscow building, smashing windows and breaking down doors. Boris was inside resisting eviction, helped by workers who threw bottles of vodka at the police. Despite his wife suffering a head injury, Boris only gave up after a lengthy struggle.

The reuse for its original purpose of "the house by the Cast Iron

Bridge", once the pride of Pyotr Arsenijevic Smirnov, was short-lived, but the wily old founder would have admired Boris for his tenacity whilst at the same time deploring his mistaken judgement.

Perhaps rather surprisingly, the most popular way of enjoying vodka in the West has now begun to influence the drinkers in the countries who first produced it. With the greater ability to travel abroad since the collapse of Communism, young drinkers in Poland have been influenced by western fashions and are drinking flavoured vodka in increasing numbers, with lemon proving to be the most popular variant. If they were considered slow to adopt western drinking habits, this is partly because outdoor and internet alcohol advertising is not allowed in Poland.

Drinking trends in Russia have changed in recent years and vary across the country. Outside the two main cities of St. Petersburg and Moscow, the straight vodka shot is still preferred above all other alcoholic drinks. The fashion-conscious in Moscow prefer to drink whisky, rum and tequila instead of neat vodka, as they consider themselves more international by doing so. If they drink vodka at all, it is in a cocktail because it is considered "the international way of drinking vodka". According to one trade magazine, the cocktail culture is expanding rapidly in St. Petersburg, "which follows trends established in Moscow, such as the popularity of the fruit cocktails, while Moscow follows what's happening in the UK."

It is however unlikely that either Russia or Poland will follow the UK's most recent trend of vodka production in the form of speciality distilling on a small scale, sometimes described as "organic distilling". New arrivals in the UK vodka market have concentrated on small but quality-controlled production for a speciality market, which deliberately makes no effort to compete with more famous brands. The advertising language used by the small producer is unashamedly chosen to appeal to the type of middle-class consumers who are more likely to buy produce from farmers' markets.

Two such London vodka companies have gained particularly high praise: Sipsmith of Hammersmith and Sacred Vodka in Highgate. Both firms have employed different methods of distillation. The first handmade copper-pot still to be made in London for 189 years produces small batches of vodka from barley grain for Sipsmith in an extremely labour-intensive process. The language Sipsmith uses – "crafting truly artisanal spirits of uncompromising quality" – is chosen to reinforce the suggestion that their products are given the same care and individual treatment you would expect from makers of custom-made furniture rather than a mass-produced factory object.

Its founder, Fairfax Hall, claims that vodka drinkers are "tired of the message dripping off vodka packaging that one brand is more expensive than another or confers more status", and believes that in the future "people will move away from consuming vodka for status or as a mixer and will begin to focus on its taste. This will lead to higher-quality, taste-oriented cocktails based on craft vodka, for the more discerning drinker."

Alex Kammerling, who used to work for Grey Goose, has commented that when selling vodka:

> The story and quality are obviously key these days. People want artisanal. Look at something like Sipsmith with a beautiful little still in a residential area of West London that produces a great spirit. It has a great story, but what's interesting is looking at how these and other distillers deal with demand. If they exceed capacity and have to distil somewhere else, do you lose a bit of the romanticism?

By contrast, the Highgate Distillery uses a completely different method of distillation with the aid of its Sacred Microdistillery equipment, which also produces a gin. Both of the firm's vodka and gin products use English grain spirit, but the inclusion of "botanicals", a flavouring process more generally reserved for gin, is also used for their vodka.

That the small producer can succeed in terms of international recognition when judged alongside mass-market names was proved by William Chase when his Chase Vodka won the 2010 San Francisco World Spirits Competition. Chase, who started distilling the vodka in 2008, had previously made Tyrells crisps, and his Hereford farm potatoes were the natural choice for the vodka's basic raw ingredient. Thirty-five pounds of potatoes are needed to produce just one bottle, but the result is a creamy vodka often preferred by those who would rather sip the spirit than drink it in one shot.

At one time out of fashion in the UK, the vodka cocktail has been restored to favour in the last few years, largely through specialist vodka bars which also devise evenings of entertainment. Vodka's qualities, its effectiveness as a good mixer and the fact that it was drunk in large quantities by young drinkers, inspired the three owners of Inventive Leisure to create a bar dedicated to vodka, which would offer a large choice of the spirit. They took Irish pubs as their model for their Revolution bar chain. Those pubs, with their old-fashioned decor, traditional seating, good food and Irish stout, appeared to succeed in attracting like-minded drinkers who sought the same features. Despite being themed, Irish bars were genuine rather than gimmicky places to socialise in.

Revolution bars aimed to provide a similar ambiance for vodka drinkers and consequently included interior furnishings of red velvet curtains and artwork suggestive of both Imperial and Soviet Russia. The atmosphere was comfortable and friendly, and the first Revolution bar, which opened in Manchester in 1996, was aimed at the student drinker and offered a completely new vodka experience.

Revolution's trademark speciality, the flavoured shot, was an immediate success. Over thirty varieties with a base of Absolut vodka were bottled in a vodka factory in Dukinfield near Manchester. An early "mint chocolate shot" did not see vodka being soaked in polo mints, as some bars had provided, but instead used Aero mint chocolate. Served ice cold, new variants such as Bakewell Tart and Turkish Delight drew on favourites of the cake or sweet shop, but the flavours changed with the seasons and even included Mince Pie and Cream.

From the outset, Revolution sold over fifty premium brands of vodka, with Stolichnaya later being replaced by Eristoff as the house brand. Most of the vodkas were unfamiliar not only to the potential customers but also to some of the bar staff who could not pronounce all of the names. It was then that Revolution employed vodka experts to train their staff and to encourage customers to take part in tasting sessions so that they knew their Ketel One Citroen from their Grey Goose Le Citron.

As Revolution grew, its target market expanded beyond the student drinker, and at the time of writing there are sixty-one Revolution vodka bars from Aberdeen to Plymouth, which also sell food, wine and beer.

There is one Revolution bar in the UK, located in Manchester, which is student-only, but it is not the original flagship bar. Even there, the velvet curtains and the Russian-inspired art fittings have gone, as the Revolution style has now adapted to suit the areas where the bars are situated and the consumers who drink in them. Although not a vodka club, Revolution comes closest to those found in Russia and Poland. Free privilege cards qualify their holders for special concessions, free drinks and other packages that are centred around the concept of sharing vodka with friends. Only in Edinburgh is there a nightclub dedicated to vodka. Red Vodka Club is situated in the heart of the city's clubland and serves over sixty premium vodkas as well as beer and other drinks.

Given the size of the country, it is risky to state that the most remarkable venue for drinking vodka in the US is to be found in the form of Red Square Bar in the Mandalay Bay Hotel, Las Vegas. Nevertheless, the bar has created a setting that aims to recreate the experience of drinking vodka in Imperial and Soviet Russia but in the comfort of a luxury American hotel. It claims to sell the greatest number of vodkas in America.

Emulating the post-Soviet destruction of images of Lenin, guests on the way to the bar are greeted by a headless 14 foot statue of the Soviet leader. The head of the statue used to hang from the ceiling in the bar until it mysteriously vanished in 1999. It was returned when a reward of $5,000 was offered, and it was then frozen in a solid block of ice, forming the centrepiece of the special vodka vault where the temperature is -5 degrees Fahrenheit. To endure the Siberian winter climate, visitors are lent either full-length Russian furs or military coats along with fur hats before choosing vodka from over two hundred varieties, which are served on a frozen ice bar.

In the main bar, the interior is decorated with a mixture of opulent red hangings from the Imperial years, a chandelier from a defunct Russian embassy and Soviet propaganda posters on brick walls. Vodka drinkers are encouraged to drink the shots straight in the Russian tradition and can seek assistance from a "Vodka Goddess" to enjoy the best experience the bar can provide. The restaurant also serves Russian food, wisely opting to be "*perestroika* inspired" than to take its culinary cues from Soviet-era fare.

Part 3

Drinking and Preparing Vodka

The transforming power of vodka

Soviet vodka cup – post 1917

The Pryzhov Test: A Tasting Guide

All the vodkas chosen are easily obtainable and are judged on the Pryzhov approval scale of one to five for the inclusive qualities of smoothness, taste and value.

Absolut 100 – Sweden – 50% – Winter wheat

Absolut 100 makes more sense as a product name in America than in the UK where the proof is halved.

Bottle & label: Maintaining the Absolut tradition, but the bottle is totally black.

Tasting notes: Like all Absolut vodkas, it is reliably smooth as well as being strong with a pleasant, fruity and spicy kick.

Best use: It can be used as a mixer or served straight on ice.

Pryzhov approval: 🍷🍷🍷🍷

English Spirit Vodka – England – 54% – sugar beet, water and yeast

Only the heart of the distillation is used, a factor which contributes to the small batches of fifteen bottles made from a copper-pot still. As well as their vodkas, the company makes gin and offers a service for fruit farmers to convert their produce into spirits of their choice. The company's other vodkas include Coffee Bean Vodka and English Spirit Seasonal Fruit Vodka (both 37% proof), with the latter depending on what fresh picked fruit is available. Its advertising language is strongly "artisanal".

Bottle & label: The bottle shape is reminiscent of Absolut. Crisp, clear labelling, with a flag of St. George, marks it out as an unmistakably English product.

Tasting notes: Notes of soft, warm honey and a hint of lemon make for a very clean taste. It also has a light, bready flavour.

Best use: It makes for an excellent mixer because of the high proof and is very acceptable served on ice or very cold.

Pryzhov approval : 🍷🍷🍷

Glen's Vodka – Scotland – 37.5% – sugar beet

Glen's is almost a joke to many, as it has no pretensions whatsoever and makes no claims for itself except for being "exciting".

Bottle & label: It is one of the cheapest vodkas on the market and not the worst.

Tasting notes: Its quality has astonished at least one vodka expert in blind tastings. When drunk neat, it does have a noticeable, but not aggressive, burn, which is enjoyed by some vodka drinkers. It also has a hot, citric quality when swallowed.

Best use: It is the perfect base for a concentrated fruit-flavoured mixer and for homemade herbal or fruit infusions.

Pryzhov approval: 🍷🍷🍷

Grey Goose – France – 40% – corn, rye wheat and barley

Produced in the Picardy region of France where cognac reigns, it is now one of the stars in the vodka world. It is said that Grey Goose inspired the creation of other "ultra-premium" vodkas.

Bottle & label: Each bottle is hand-made and is frosted with geese and cool mountains as well as the French tricolour.

Tasting notes: Extra smooth and dense in the mouth, Grey Goose has hints of wheat and dark chocolate.

Best use: It makes for an excellent mixer and is safe on ice.

Pryzhov approval:

Legend of Kremlin – Russia – 40% – winter wheat

It would be easy to become sentimental about this vodka, as it purports to be made from the original recipe used in 1430 by Isidor, the monk who might be described as the father of Russian vodka. Modern technology has refined away the 15th-century impurities using artesian-well water, special grain spirit and traditional copper vats.

Bottle & label: The highly distinctive, longnecked-carafe shape is based on 18th-century vodka flasks. The slightly austere label is decorated with Isidor's name.

Tasting notes: This smooth, glowing spirit is slightly musky and has hints of warm pepper and honey.

Best use: It is better straight on ice than when used as a mixer.

Pryzhov approval: 🍷🍷🍷🍷

Luksusowa – Poland – 40% – Potato

Using the same recipe since 1928, Luksusowa easily surpasses many more highly-promoted brands made from potato for all-round quality.

Bottle & label: If the content was judged by the look of the bottle, the vodka would be deemed rather lacklustre, but the brand is immediately distinctive courtesy of its red and white lettering.

Tasting notes: A rich, soft and creamy vodka, Luksusowa has a mellow sweetness, which remains after it is swallowed.

Best use: It can be used as a mixer, but the subtle flavours excel when drunk with ice.

Pryzhov approval: 🍷🍷🍷🍷🍷

Okhotnichya (Hunter's vodka) – Russia – 45% – winter wheat

More a *nastokya* than a vodka, the brand is a well-known classic. Water and port wine are added to the spirit, which is infused with spices and herbs including pepper, angelica, aniseed and juniper. Traditionally drunk in cold weather, it has a rich amber colour.

Bottle & label: Although the bottle has a plain shape, the label has elements of Soviet poster art as well as shades of orange, gold and brown. The presence of a duck on the label reinforces the hunter motif.

Tasting notes: Honey and pepper notes combine with a lingering taste of ginger to leave a hot, but not burning, sensation.

Best use: Delicious when sipped on its own.

Pryzhov approval: 🍷🍷🍷🍷

Pertsovka – Russia – 45% – Winter wheat

The vodka is infused with red and black peppers and cubeb berries (Java pepper) and is a rather vivid red in the glass.

Bottle & label: The plain bottle is redolent of the Soviet period, while the large red peppers on the label leave the temperature of the vodka in no doubt.

Tasting notes: Initially very hot and slightly bitter, it settles very quickly to leave a warm feeling.

Best use: The spirit is good when drunk neat, chilled or with ice. Although it is unlikely to be as hot as Peter the Great's favourite peppered vodka, it has a bite which makes it a good base for a Bloody Mary.

Pryzhov approval: 🍷🍷🍷🍷

Siwucha – Poland – 40 % – rye and barley

Siwucha is a curious but successful attempt to recreate a type of vodka drunk in Russia and Poland between the two world wars. The choice of name reflects Slavic humour – in Polish and Russian it means “moonshine” or even “rotgut”. Made from rye and barley, it is one of the few vodkas to be aged in oak, and the distinctive taste is created by the inclusion of sloe.

Bottle & label: The old method of sealing vodka with a cork and wax is used here, and the label for the half-litre bottle is correspondingly old-fashioned in appearance.

Tasting notes: Warm, sweet and gentle, the spirit has subtle hints of fruit.

Best use: Siwucha is best enjoyed neat and at room temperature, but does not suffer from being slightly chilled.

Pryzhov approval: 🍷🍷🍷🍷🍷

Smirnoff's Blueberry – Italy – believed to be corn – 37.5%

This vodka contains Smirnoff No 21, which has been infused with blueberries, resulting in a distinct and unusual flavour.

Tasting notes: Although slightly harsh and tingly after swallowing, the citrus taste makes the drink extremely refreshing.

Best use: This vodka can be drunk neat with ice or with a plain mixer such as lemonade.

Pryzhov approval:

Stolichnaya – Russia – 40 % – winter wheat and rye

Stolichnaya is made from Kalingrad water and filtered using traditional Russian methods. Elderly émigré Russians are fervent in their praise of Stolichnaya, insisting that it tastes of the vodka they remember in their homeland.

Bottle & label: Bottles adorned with the old-fashioned label featuring the hideous Hotel Moskva of Stalin's day can still be found, but a series of colourful new designs by Yuri Gorbachev has brought the bottle into the present day.

Tasting notes: A momentarily hot sensation is followed by lemon and bread flavours when drinking this silky vodka.

Best use: Stolichnaya is extremely versatile and can be drunk neat or used as a mixer.

Pryzhov approval: 🍷🍷🍷🍷🍷

Utkins UK5 Organic Vodka – United Kingdom – 40% – rye

Utkins UK5 is the world's first organic vodka to be made completely from rye. Although the rye comes from a German farm, which has been organic for over 30 years, the spirit is produced in Kent. Organic products do not use artificial insecticides or herbicides, and UK5 relies on the purity of the material used before the distilling process, which eliminates the need for purification by carbon filtration.

Bottle & label: The traditional bottle shape is combined with the silver and blue label, which has the Prince of Wales feathers that denote Prince Charles' seal of approval.

Tasting notes: This cool and smooth vodka is creamy and has a flavour reminiscent of baking bread flavour.

Best use: The vodka is excellent when drunk neat with ice but can also be used to make raspberry-flavoured *nalivka*.

Pryzhov approval: 🍷🍷🍷🍷🍷

Zorokovich 1917 – Ukraine – 40% – winter wheat

Like the English Spirit Vodka, only the heart of the distillation is used to create Zorokovich 1917. Although the vodka is produced on a small scale, it is not made in a copper still.

Bottle & label: The traditional bottle shape features black swallows and a tie-on tag that suggests age and maturity.

Tasting notes: Hints of aniseed and baking bread combine with suggestions of spice and nutmeg to leave a warm and pleasant aftertaste.

Best use: The spirit is very good when prepared neat on ice and also makes a good base for a Bloody Mary.

Pryzhov approval: 🍷🍷🍷🍷

Preparing Vodka

Vodka in Russia is often shared by three drinkers, a tradition started in Soviet days when a half-bottle of vodka, purchased along with a packet of processed cheese as the snack, came to a convenient three roubles. John Steinbeck was once beckoned into a doorway when in Moscow and asked to be the third drinker to share such a bottle.

An old tradition when drinking vodka was to make the sign of the cross before blowing the top of the vodka glass to banish the devil, which sits on top of the vodka.

Even in the cheapest Russian pubs, vodka is never served without the accompaniment of the traditional *zakuski.* At the very least this will include bread with small pickled cucumbers, but it may involve more elaborate meat or fish snacks.

Vodka should be laid out at room temperature and should be poured into a shot glass. If poured into a large glass, the smell, an important part of the tasting experience, is lost. Vodka is judged by its smell, taste and finish. The latter is sometimes known as "the burn" or the sensation experienced when the spirit is swallowed. If the vodka is of a good quality, there should be no lingering sense of "burning" when it is swallowed slowly.

Vodka Cocktails and Vodka Recipes

Cocktails and other vodka-based drinks

The simple guidelines below will ensure the best results when using vodka in cocktails:

Mixing – If using a cocktail shaker, always put the ice in the shaker first and the vodka last.

Stirring – A drink that is stirred will pour relatively clearly when strained and should have no fragments of ice.

Shaking – Shake the drink to mix the ingredients if they include thickeners such as cream, egg or juices.

As a hangover cure, the Bloody Mary has acquired a legendary curative power, but a variant of the classic recipe provided by occult author Dennis Wheatley is unusual for including Campbell's beef bouillon. This appears never to have been made, and Wheatley probably meant to use their consommé, which would be rather rich but delicious. (Campbell's products are currently relicensed to Batchelors in the UK.)

Dennis Wheatley's Bloody Mary:
1 nip tomato juice, 1 sherry glass Smirnoff vodka, 1 sherry glass Batchelors/Campbell's beef consommé, 1 nip Worcestershire Sauce, a half glass of fresh lime or lemon, ice. Shake until froth appears and serve.

Petiot's Bloody Mary:
4 large dashes of salt, 2 dashes of black pepper, 2 dashes of cayenne pepper, a layer of Worcestershire Sauce, a dash of lemon juice, cracked ice, 2 ounces [almost 4 tablespoons] of vodka and 2 ounces of thick tomato juice.
Shake, strain and pour.

Note that the original recipe above has no Tabasco Sauce, horseradish, celery or salt and is not garnished with a stick of celery.

Beef bouillon is the essential ingredient, along with vodka, to make Bullshot, a hangover cure, but one which does not contain tomato juice. Do not over-chill the beef bouillon as it will set like jelly.

Bullshot:
1 measure vodka, 1 measure beef bouillon, chilled (if Campbells/Batchelors is used), juice of ½ a lemon, 1 dash Worcestershire Sauce, 1 dash Tabasco Sauce, ice and salt to taste.
Shake and serve.

Before the Bloody Mary appeared, the earliest published vodka cocktails in America were printed in 1934:

Bee's Knees Cocktail:
Dissolve 1 part honey by thoroughly stirring in one part lime juice. Then add 4 to 5 parts vodka.
Shake well.

Tsarina Cocktail:
1 part pineapple juice, 1 part vodka, add a dash of bitters if desired.
Shake.

Vodka Perfect Cocktail:

3 parts vodka, ½ part Italian vermouth,
½ French vermouth, twist of lemon peel.
Stir and strain.

Vodka Queen Cocktail:
2 parts vodka, 1 part Benedictine, 1 dash bitters.
Shake.

Tout-de-suite:
1 part Creme de Cacao, 1 part dry gin, 1 part vodka.
Shake.

Volga:
2 parts vodka, 1 part lemon juice, 1 part orange juice, dash of bitters, two dashes of Grenadine.

Here is the recipe inspired by the British television comedy *Absolutely Fabulous*.

Absolutely Fabulous cocktail:
Shake 30 ml of Stolichnaya vodka and 60 ml of cranberry juice with ice and strain into flute glass. Top up with Bollinger champagne and garnish the glass rim with strawberry. Less expensive brands of champagne and vodka can be substituted. The result may be less fabulous but will still be enjoyable.

The flavoured vodkas of Imperial Russia were extremely popular and were collectively known as *nastoykas*. The sweeter infusions such as raspberry and rowanberry were called *nalivkas*. Any fruit can be used, but raspberry is one of the best. The process of using fresh fruit described below takes a matter of weeks. If you are unable to wait that long, neutral vodka can be flavoured to taste with a variety of extremely good fruit syrups found in Polish delicatessens and some supermarkets under the brand names of Herbapol and Lowicz.

The *nalivka* is made in two stages. The first sees fresh raspberries being infused in vodka, and the second involves combining the infusion with bar syrup.

Raspberry nalivka:

Equipment: small pan, wooden spoon, large bowl, coffee filters, sieve, large glass jar with tight screw lid, small glass jar with screw lid.

Ingredients:
Infusion: 1 kg of raspberries, 750 ml of vodka.
Bar Syrup: 200 g (7 oz) of sugar, 200 ml of water, 60 ml of vodka (about three tablespoons).

Method for the syrup:
First boil the water and stir in the sugar to make the bar syrup. When the sugar has dissolved, turn down the heat and simmer gently until the syrup has thickened slightly, and remove from the heat. When the syrup has cooled, stir in the 60 ml of vodka and pour into the small glass jar. Seal with screw-top lid and set aside.

Method for the infusion:
Place the raspberries in the bowl and squash with the spoon into a mash. Transfer the raspberries with the juice into the glass jar, add the vodka and seal with the screw lid. Shake the jar to distribute the vodka and set aside in a cupboard for two months in order to avoid sunlight. Periodically give the jar a good shake before returning it to the cupboard. When the two months have elapsed, pour the contents of the jar through a small sieve into the bowl and dispose of the fruit. Thoroughly wash out the now empty jar. Open out a large coffee filter, dampen it with cold water and place the filter into the sieve. (If a coffee filter is not available, shape a double layer of kitchen towel into the sieve instead. A fine net gauze typically

used for jam-making can also be employed.) Strain the liquid through the lined sieve or gauze back into the jar in small batches while taking care not to flood the sieve. Finally, add the bar syrup into the large jar with the liquid and stir to blend before pouring contents into a glass bottle with screw top. Leave for one week before drinking.

Vodka Jelly Shots
Vodka jelly varies depending on the proportion of vodka to water and the chosen flavour.

Ingredients and equipment:
1 bottle of neutral, clear vodka. Supermarket brands, especially the extremely drinkable Lidl's Putinoff, are perfect here.
1 packet of table jelly with your preferred flavour, a bowl, a fork, 6 shot glasses.
8 ounces (227 ml) of boiling water.

Method:
Boil water and pour on jelly, stirring with fork until all the jelly is dissolved, ensuring there are no lumps of solid jelly.
Let jelly and water mixture cool a little, before adding 10 ounces of vodka (284 ml).
Pour into shot glasses and chill in refrigerator until set.

Vodka in Food

In a booklet published in the late 1950s, Smirnoff suggested cooking with vodka, but its recipes were limited to flambé chicken and meats.

A recent Thanksgiving recipe for making turkey especially succulent was prepared by a New York pub and involves injecting the twenty-pound birds with eight ounces of vodka over a three-day period, using an eight-inch syringe. By the time the bird was cooked, most of the vodka had evaporated in the oven, but diners reported that it was the most interesting and tastiest turkey they had ever eaten.

One recipe using vodka in a pasta sauce has evolved into a classic. Below is a version from the north of Italy:

Specialità Pasta Vodka Della Contessa Paola – serves four.
Ingredients:
1 tablespoon of butter
1 tablespoon of olive oil
2 cloves of garlic, finely chopped
2 medium onions, finely chopped
2 tablespoons of basil leaves (2 teaspoons if dried)
1 tablespoon of tarragon (1 teaspoon if dried)
Grated zest of 1 lemon and the juice of half a lemon.
1 quarter pint of vegetable stock
2 tins of plum tomatoes (800 g or 1.76 lbs) broken up with fork or given a quick swirl in a food processor
Half a pound of mushrooms sliced thinly
16 ounces of pasta such as penne rigate or fusilli
2 tablespoons of vodka
1 small carton of single cream or crème fraîche

Method for the sauce:
Heat a non-stick pan over a medium heat. Add butter, oil, garlic, onions, sliced mushrooms and gently sweat until soft. Add the tomatoes and herbs, half-cover with the lid and stir occasionally. Simmer very gently for half an hour, then remove from the heat. Allow to cool slightly, then stir in the single cream or crème fraîche.

Method for the pasta:
While the sauce is cooking, add the pasta to a large pan of boiling water along with a small sprinkling of salt, making sure there is room for the pasta to swell. When the pasta is

ready, turn off the heat, drain at once, return to the pan, then add half a tablespoon of butter and stir through the pasta in order to prevent it from sticking. Turn the heat to medium high, combine the cooked sauce with the pasta and stir the vodka into the pan over the heat. Remove from the heat when it begins to bubble gently – otherwise the vodka will be boiled off. If possible, serve on hot dinner plates and scatter grated parmesan on the top. Freshly-ground black pepper should be added to the individual servings and not be cooked in the sauce, as this would give it a bitter taste. The vodka is added to the sauce because the alcohol helps to release the flavour of the tomato without adding any other flavour, which would occur with the use of wine.

A vodka cup – 1770

Vodka Drinking Vessels

The Charka

The *charka* is a vodka cup in Russia and was a standardised measure of vodka in the 16th century. Its 143.5 ml size was reduced to 123 ml in 1894 to reflect the fact that changes in the law had strengthened the alcohol content of vodka.

Many of the terms associated with vodka – whether pail, bucket (*vedro*), *kovsch*, and *charka* – are centuries old and inseparable from vodka rituals. From 1531 the bucket used to measure vodka contained one hundred *charka*. The *charka* was not just confined to the tavern, nor was the *kovsch* ("scoop") only used to take vodka from a bucket. In the 17th and 18th century, the *kovsch* held about three charka or about 500 to 600 ml. In the 19th century, this measure was transformed into the vodka bottle of 610 ml.

Because vodka was drunk by all classes, the material used to fashion the *charka* would reflect the wealth of the household. The most expensive were made of gold or silver and have changed their form over the years. Each reign and period has given them a distinctive shape with the result that baroque, classical and pan-Slavonic designs were all created.

The early 17th-century *charkas* were usually large and shallow, reflecting the weakness of the vodka, which had a proof of 15 to 20 per cent. As distilling developed, vodka became stronger and the *charkas* became smaller. The late 17th-century *charkas* can be divided into several distinct types. Common features found in all *charkas* are the flat, horizontal handle and the presence of either one foot or three feet. The earliest models, probably dating from the third quarter of the century, were usually unmarked cups, often semispherical or shallow in shape.

Perhaps the most common *charka* during this time was a cup with one foot and a horizontal handle. It was decorated with large birds and sea monsters such as Jonah and the whale. Only a limited number of *charkas* exist from the first quarter of the 18th century. The style changed at the turn of the century and the *charkas* began to resemble traditional goblets. The most common shape of the 18th century mimicked a thistle flower and often had a scroll handle attached to it in a vertical position.

From the early 19th century, glass replaced silver as the material of drinking vessels, and there are few *charkas* from that period. Later in the 19th century, rich pan-Slavonic design predominated. Other vodka cups were miniature silver replicas of regimental headgear, but because they could not be put down on the table due to their shape, the vodka had to be drunk *do dnia* or "to the bottom".

At the turn of the 20th century, the silversmith's art reached a new level when several suppliers to the Imperial Court, such as Fabergé, Khlebnikov and Ovchinnikov, created *charka* and other vodka-container masterpieces in enamel, gold or silver. The Soviet regime allowed their sale as second-hand items but not before adding Soviet silver marks and obliterating the stamped Imperial double eagle originally allowed to identify suppliers to the Imperial Court. Vodka cups continued to be made in silver, even in Soviet times, and were either plain silver or decorated with enamel.

The Kovsch

The *kovsch* was originally made of wood. A deep spoon or ladle with a flat bottom, it conveyed vodka from a barrel or bucket. By the 16th century, a boat shape often made in wood had evolved in the north of Russia and was carved to resemble various water fowl. When made in precious metals, the *kovsch* was highly decorated, often with flowers, leaves and animals. Before the introduction of medallions, it was a traditional gift given to foreign dignitaries by the tsar. Various shapes and sizes were used when the kovsch became a part of ceremonies such as funerals and weddings. By the late 19th century, the *kovsch*, made in silver and enamel as a purely decorative object, had often become a vulgar, over-elaborate showpiece of the silversmiths' art.

Extract from *The Siren's Song*, by Anton Chekhov

When you come in the table must be set, and when you sit down you tuck the napkin into your collar and you take your time about reaching for the vodka decanter. And mind you, you don't pour it into an ordinary wine glass, you don't treat a sweetheart that way! No. You pour it into something antique, made of silver, an heirloom, or into a quaint pot-bellied little glass with an inscription on it, something like this: 'As you clink, you may think, monks also thus do drink.' And you don't gulp it straight off, but first you gaze nonchalantly at the ceiling, and only then, slowly you raise it to your lips, and at once sparks from your stomach flash through your whole body.

Part 4

Literature, Music and Vodka

Literature cashing in on the rising popularity of vodka in America in 1957

Leo Tolstoy

Fyodor Dostoevsky

Russian Writers

I

Tolstoy, Dostoevsky and Pryzhov

When he was young, Tolstoy led a rake's life, or as he put it himself in *A Confession*: "I fornicated and practised deceit. Lying, thieving, promiscuity of all kinds, drunkenness, violence, murder… there was not one crime I did not commit." (The "murder" refers to his time as a soldier in the army.)

Tolstoy recalled enjoying vodka when he was a student, but in his middle-age he repented and regretted all the follies of his youth. By the time he was sixty, he became obsessed with alcohol abstention, not simply moderation.

Before the state even considered a national temperance movement, Tolstoy founded his own temperance society called the Union Against Drunkenness in 1887. He did not have just the lower classes in his sights, for Tolstoy stressed that the whole nation, regardless of class, had to give up alcohol, an admonition he repeated in 1889 for the benefit of the members of the intelligentsia who had drunk gallons of vodka and behaved badly on the Foundation Day of Moscow University. The student drinking on that day was so colossal that Chekhov said that they drank everything in Moscow and would have drained the river if it had not been frozen.

When Tolstoy's polemic was read by the students of another university, they dismissed his advice by proposing a toast to his health with the aid of large tumblers of vodka. They then published an account of their activities in a local newspaper to make sure that the old man heard about their Tolstoy-inspired jollies. They remarked that they were young and wanted to enjoy themselves, but that they might consider giving up alcohol when they were old like Tolstoy.

Tolstoy's views on alcohol were only one part of a new philosophy he adopted from the late 1880s when he underwent a kind of religious conversion during which he gave up all of his vices and became a vegetarian.

The mentions of vodka in *War and Peace* and *Anna Karenina* are very few considering the length of the books but occur more frequently in his short stories in which he is sometimes judgmental. Tolstoy more often introduces vodka as a feature of normal domestic or military Russian life, and when he is not being dogmatic, vodka accompanies lively humour in his fiction.

His own moment of revelation about the power of alcohol had come to him when he overheard a cab driver discussing a crime, saying, "it would be a shame to do that if one were not drunk". He related a true story:

> I remember being struck by the evidence of a cook who was tried for murdering a relation of mine, an old lady in whose service he lived. He… wished to go into the bedroom with a knife, but felt that while sober he could not commit the deed he had planned… [because] "when a man's sober, he's ashamed". He turned back, drank two tumblers of vodka he had prepared beforehand, and only then felt himself ready, and committed the crime…

Tolstoy wrote a play called *The First Distiller*, which was a dramatisation of his short story *How the Devil Earned His First Bread*, an adaptation of a folk tale. The play, first staged in an open-air theatre near a worker's factory outside St. Petersburg in 1886, depicts the devil arranging for a peasant to have a surplus of grain at harvest, which at the devil's suggestion he converts into vodka. After a few bottles of vodka have been drunk, those knocking it back become as wild as beasts, ignoring the earlier entreaties of an old man to leave it alone. Intended as a play for the masses, it was so successful that the censor banned further performances of similar plays.

Despite his public views on alcohol, Tolstoy allowed it in his own house, and for the effects of drunkenness, he needed to look no further than his son Ilya. Sofia, Tolstoy's much put-upon wife, noted in her diary in 1897 that she warned him and two of his brothers about "the evils of alcohol, strongly urging them not to touch it", a plea that went unheeded. Although his children were permitted to drink alcohol, when a group of actors arrived to rehearse a play in Tolstoy's house in Yasnaya Polyana, they found that the fulsome welcome they were given did not extend to strong drink:

> A well-spread supper table awaited us. But intoxicants were conspicuously absent, their place being ostentatiously taken by decanters of *kvas* [a very weak home-made beer]. We, frozen travellers, experienced a feeling akin to disillusionment; but the foresight of one of our party had secured a supply… of what was not allowed at Yasnaya, and we escaped cautiously, in turn, to the entrance hall, and there, in a corner under the stairs (feeling the gnawings of conscience) we warmed ourselves with drams of vodka.

Despite Tolstoy's disapproval of alcohol, one of his early biographers remembered a walk with the author who "showed how much he sympathised with tipsy peasants. Tolstoy remarked, 'Ah! But you should see how affectionate they are in their cups. Their fundamental good nature shows itself then. They are full of kindliness and want to embrace you, and are ready to give their souls to serve you.'"

Tolstoy's sympathies were demonstrated when he recovered land for some peasants that had been stolen from their commune. They thanked him by harvesting his own fields, intending to work for nothing. But Tolstoy paid them well, rewarding the peasants with a dinner and supplies of vodka. However much he was against vodka, as a landowner Tolstoy knew that he had to uphold the traditions that were associated with harvesting.

It was the peasant's desire for a particular enamel cup, which became known as the "Blood Cup", which Tolstoy was particularly scathing about, because it was associated with free vodka and beer. It featured when half a million people gathered to celebrate the coronation of Nicholas II in 1896 in the Khodinka field near Moscow. When a signal was given that the free gifts including food and vodka were ready for the taking, the crowd surged forward. Due to bad planning by the organisers, several thousand people were crushed to death in the ensuing stampede.

Tolstoy had condemned the coronation for being "terrible in its absurdity and an insane waste of money" and attacked the young tsar for declaring he would uphold the autocracy of his father. It was uncharacteristically unreasonable of Tolstoy to rebuke the poor for the tragic fiasco when he concluded that it was "quite clear that only those were guilty [who] rushed forward in order to get a piece of cake and a glass of vodka."

Two years before the coronation, he had written a story about Nicholas II's accession to the throne called *The Young Tsar* in which changes for the betterment of the population come to the monarch in a dream. The surprisingly policy-heavy dream includes the relinquishing of control of the tsar's taverns. It could not be published, but Tolstoy would later redouble his obsession with teetotalism when the state gained complete control of vodka.

He corresponded with Michael Chelysev, the deputy who had spoken at the 1905 *duma*, who was, like him, a fervent campaigner for total abstinence. In 1909, in one of his last acts, Tolstoy sent a drawing at Chelysev's request to be used on the labels of all vodka bottles. *The Guardian* newspaper reported in the previous year that the *duma* had voted "in favour or removing the Imperial Eagle from the labels of vodka bottles and substituting a skull and cross-bones denoting poison; with appropriate warnings against overindulgence."

Tolstoy posted his drawing, which is still preserved, but for reasons which are unclear, no such label was ever officially used. The health warning would wait nearly a hundred years before it was widely adopted, but a temperance society label with the Tolstoy design circulated in parts of Russia.

Abandoning poor Sofia, Tolstoy took himself off like an elephant seeking its secret graveyard and became ill at a railway station, where he died in the company of a male secretary. Ten days before, he wrote to his daughter Alexandra, asking for some books including the second volume of Dostoevsky's *The Brothers Karamazov*.

The two writers never met, and although Dostoevsky admired Tolstoy, the older writer professed to dislike his compatriot's work. As far as vodka abstinence was concerned, their views diverged. But in his *Writer's Diary*, Dostoevsky relayed how he had been incensed by the cruelty meted out to a horse when he was a young man waiting for a coach to take him to St. Petersburg. He laid the blame squarely at the foot of vodka:

> Directly across the street from the inn was the station building. Suddenly a courier's troika came flying up to the station entrance and a government courier leapt out… I recall that our driver said that such couriers always drink a glass of vodka at every station, since without it they couldn't stand up to "the punishment they have to take". In the meantime a new troika of fresh, spirited horses rolled up to the station and the coachman, a young lad of twenty or so, wearing a red shirt and carrying his coat on his arm, jumped onto the seat. The courier at once flew out of the inn, ran down the steps, and got into the carriage. Before the coachman could even start the horses, the courier stood up and, silently, without any word whatsoever, raised his huge right fist and dealt a painful blow straight down on the back of the coachman's neck. The coachman jolted forward, raised his whip, and lashed the shaft horse with all his might. The horses started off with a rush, but this did nothing to appease the courier. He was not angry; he was acting according to his own plan… and the terrible fist was raised again, and again it struck the coachman's neck, and then again and again; and so it continued until the troika

disappeared from sight. Naturally the coachman, who could barely hold on because of the blows, kept lashing the horses every second like one gone mad; and at last his blows made the horses fly off as if possessed. Our coachman explained to me that all government couriers travel in almost the same fashion and that this particular one was universally known for it; once he had had his vodka and jumped into the carriage, he would always begin by beating, "always in that same way", for no reason whatsoever; he would beat in a measured manner, raising and lowering his fist, and "he'll keep using his fists on the coachman like that for nearly a mile, and then he'll quit. And if he gets to feeling bored, he might take it up again in the middle of the trip…"
I could never forget the courier, and for a long time thereafter I couldn't help but explain many of the shameful and cruel things about the Russian People in too one-sided a manner. …the courier is gone, but on the other hand there is "demon-vodka".

In what way can demon-vodka resemble the courier? It can do so very easily in the way it coarsens and brutalises a man, makes him callous, and turns him away from clear thinking, desensitises him to the power of goodness. A drunkard doesn't care about kindness to animals; a drunkard will abandon his wife and children. A drunken man came to the wife he had abandoned and whom, along with her children, he had not supported for many months; he demanded vodka and set to beating her to force her to give him still more vodka; the unfortunate woman, compelled to virtual forced labour (just recall what women's work is and what value we place on it now) and not knowing how to feed her children, seized a knife and stabbed him. This happened recently, and she will be brought to trial… there are hundreds and thousands of such cases – just open a newspaper. But the chief similarity between demon-vodka and the courier is certainly that it, just as fatally and irresistibly, towers over the human will.

> …A fire broke out in a village; there was a church in the village, but the tavern keeper came out and shouted that if the villagers abandoned the church and saved his tavern, he would stand them a barrel of vodka. The church burned down, but the tavern was saved. These instances are still trivial compared with the countless horrors yet to come.

Dostoevsky reserved many passages of invective about vodka for his *Writer's Diary,* but modified them for his novels. Excessive drinking was not amongst Dostoevsky's vices although gambling was, and he famously begged on his knees for his wife to hand over her wedding ring to finance his habit. He wrote to a strict daily timetable, which allowed him to receive visitors in the afternoon before enjoying a light meal at three o'clock. Dostoevsky always drank a glass of vodka with it, nibbling a slice of black bread between sips, which he believed was the healthiest way to enjoy the spirit.

When Dostoevsky was imprisoned in Siberia, health was the last consideration for the prisoners who overcame their revulsion at the way vodka was smuggled in. A convict working outside wrapped the vodka-filled intestines of a bullock round his body, over which he arranged his clothes in the hope that the guard would not carry out a body search.

While Dostoevsky was abroad, a sensational crime occurred in Moscow that he followed in the newspapers, as did most of literate Russia. In the early evening dark of 21 November 1869, five members of a revolutionary group known as the "People's Vengeance" made their way to a Moscow park. They intended to meet a former member, Ivan Ivanovich Ivanov, an agricultural student who had agreed to help retrieve a printing press hidden in the park near a frozen pond. The leader of the group, Sergei Nechaev, was a fanatic who had quarrelled with Ivanov and, fearing betrayal, planned to murder him.

The accomplices would have set off earlier, but they were delayed because the oldest of the conspirators, the writer Ivan Gavrilovich Pryzhov, unable to contemplate the horrors that were to come without fortification, stopped at a tavern for a generous drink of vodka. A self-confessed alcoholic, Pryzhov was something of an expert on taverns, for he had published the only book on the history of the Russian tavern in 1868.

As soon as Ivanov arrived, the gang emerged from a grotto. Nechaev first tried to strangle the student before opting to shoot him through the head. The body was stripped of all traces of the victim's identity and forced through a hole in the pond. The conspirators then hurried to a safe house where Nechaev changed out of his blood-stained shirt. He fired at Pryzhov with his gun, narrowly missing his head.

Pryzhov had no doubt that it was not an accident, for he had argued with Nechaev that morning, telling him that he was mad to even think of committing murder. He had tried not to be involved at all. Aged forty-two and twice as old as the others, he was lame and could not see in the dark. Nechaev dismissed his excuses, and Pryzhov was told that he would have to take part – even if he had to be carried to the park.

The body was discovered a few days later. By sheer chance, the police found a list of conspirators and raided their homes. Perhaps anticipating arrest, Pryzhov burned the unpublished material he had compiled on the Russian tavern. The following day, when the police burst into Pryzhov's Moscow apartment, they grabbed his old trembling dog, which they threw across the room. It ran off and was never seen again. With the exception of Nechaev who escaped to Switzerland, the conspirators were all arrested. Nechaev would later be caught and extradited to Russia in 1872.

Pryzhov spent one and a half years awaiting trial in the Peter and Paul Fortress island at St Petersburg. He had a nervous breakdown while he was there, partially losing his memory. He had prepared a document, "Confessions", which was read in evidence in court and included a remark that his "whole life had been a dog's life" and because of Nechaev he would also "die as a dog". Pryzhov's lawyer told the court that he was a very unwilling participant in the crime, had only been there because he was threatened and took no part in the murder itself. Stammering and confused, Pryzhov repeatedly told the court that he had made a life study of the Russian people, as if this somehow justified his crimes. He rambled endlessly, blaming his appearance in the dock on society, the injustice of life, Nechaev and many others.

The court was unimpressed, and Pryzhov was sentenced to death. An avowed atheist, he declined the final prayer offered by a priest when he was climbing the steps to the gallows. At the very last moment, he was unexpectedly reprieved and sentenced instead to 12 years hard labour in Siberia, where he was to be exiled for life.

His wife Olga volunteered to go to Siberia with him. She later petitioned the tsar, explaining that her husband's health was poor and his involvement in the murder had been slight, but her pleas to release him were ignored. When his sentence ended, Pryzhov had only a few years before he died in Siberian exile in 1885. He continued to write to the end, as angry and unforgiving about life as ever.

The Nechaev affair was a *cause célèbre* in its day, and as information came to light about the crime and its perpetrators, the newspapers published as many details as they were allowed. Pryzhov was tall, bespectacled and had a scrawny beard as well as a permanently nervous stare. He appeared to be an unlikely criminal, but he was not spared publicity. The type of books Pryzhov had published on taverns and the dregs of society confirmed his wickedness to the press. If he had been at all a man, it was charged, he would have prevented the murder, as he was so much older than the other conspirators.

It took many years before it was realised that Pryzhov had made one of the most important contributions to the history of vodka in his *History of Taverns in Russia in connection with the History of the Russian People.* It was the only book to chart the spirit's fiery progress from its earliest years in different regions of Russia and Ukraine. It did so in minute detail and was originally conceived as a three volume work. The later works would have covered "the urban drunks, fugitives, thieves and rebels, ordinary people of no official importance", subjects which no publisher would consider.

For one who had little formal education, his book was a

remarkable achievement. Denied a place at Moscow University to study history, he was accepted as a student there under the guise of studying medicine, a subject in which he had no interest. After two years he was sent down for failing his exams, but he somehow managed to stay on and attend history lectures. Eventually he worked as a civil servant, but this ended through no fault of his own, and Pryzhov never found steady employment again.

He often drank when he was working and frequently found himself in his favourite Moscow tavern with vodka as his companion. Depression and poverty were constant features in his life, and he was probably drunk when he tried to drown himself and his dog Leporello, only for a passer-by to rescue them both. Pryzhov was only really comfortable with those he met in taverns and was motivated by bitterness at their shared oppression to write his *History of Taverns in Russia.* He felt that his situation was little different from the earliest times in Russia when the downtrodden peasants were forced by law to drink in the tsar's taverns until vodka-drinking descended down through the generations to become an accepted habit of the nation.

The book is marred by the author blaming Jewish vodka traders for selling the spirit – a common attitude then but also reflecting the writer's fondness for scapegoats. Pryzhov was in rags when he brought the manuscript to a Moscow publisher who was astonished that the man he supposed to be a vagrant had actually written it. A few days later, he accepted the book, paying Pryzhov two hundred and fifty roubles, most of which went towards paying old debts. (Unfortunately, most of the copies were destroyed in a warehouse fire, and the book was not reprinted until 1914.) In 1868, his next major project, *The Dog in the History of Human Belief*, failed to find a publisher. In a last, desperate measure, he sold off his library to a Moscow bookshop where he met a revolutionary who fatefully introduced him to Nechaev.

Pryzhov seemed to Nechaev to be the ideal person to distribute leaflets and recruit members for his anarchist group, for the writer was such a well-known frequenter of taverns in the slummy Khitrov market area of Moscow that his presence there was beyond suspicion. Pryzhov accepted Nechaev's passionate and largely mendacious account of himself, gullibly believing that the anarchist could achieve great things.

Pryzhov's father had a distinguished war record and was decorated with an honour that accorded him the status of minor nobility, a position he never used to his advantage. He was therefore unable to advance his son in society, retiring as a doorkeeper to the Moscow Hospital For The Poor where he was on good terms with Dostoevsky's surgeon father who worked there. (When the latter was allegedly murdered by his own serfs, it was rumoured they had force-fed him vodka until he drowned in it.)

Pryzhov was born in the hospital in 1827, as was the novelist six years earlier. But due to their age and social differences, they were never friends – though it is speculated that they knew each other as children. More fortunate than Pryzhov, the novelist was able to return from his own period of exile in Siberia after being sentenced to four years there for being a member of an intellectual liberal organisation. But like Pryzhov, he had known the horror of the last minute reprieve before execution.

Dostoevsky would base part of his novel, *The Devils*, on the murder and its protagonists including Pryzhov. One character in the novel reflects Pryzhov's views such as, "Seas and oceans of vodka are drunk up to support the budget", while another remarks:

> The Russian God has already given up when it comes to cheap booze. The common people are drunk, the children are drunk, the churches are empty, and in the court it's "either two hundred lashes, or bring us a bucketful of vodka".

In *Crime and Punishment*, Katerina Ivanovna was based on a charlatan beggar of whom Pryzhov had written in his book, *Beggars in Holy Russia*, published in 1860. Most of the beggars in Pryzhov's account are motivated by greed for vodka, including one Evdokiia, who is always to be found in the same district of Moscow stopping any passer-by to ask:

> "Dear brother," or "Dear sister, you can be blessed for a kopek." If she gets the kopek, she'll bless the donor, but if not, she'll send them to hell, and you know how they're afraid of these things… When someone invites her in, she sits down on the floor and starts telling tales of apparitions and visions she has seen, after which she'll ask for some vodka…

Although Pryzhov seemed destined to be remembered only as a failed revolutionary, the importance of his book on Russian taverns has been recognised as a key document of Russian history. Due to inefficient archive spring-cleaning, his manuscripts have recently turned up in odd places, surviving not because they were considered of interest but because no one could be bothered to throw them out. Still regarded by some as a mere eccentric, Pryzhov features as the subject of sympathetic research by a fictional character in a novella, *Long Goodbye*, by the 20th-century Russian writer Yury Trifonov, who says of Pryzhov that he:

> …was willing to sell his manuscripts for a glass of vodka… he was a completely useless character long forgotten by everyone, an unsuccessful rebel, a historian, a drunkard and a parasite, and at the same time a man of great nobility of character.

Ivan Pryzhov

II

Anton Chekhov

Who keeps the tavern and makes the people drunken? A peasant. Who wastes and spends on drink the funds of the commune, of the schools, of the church? A peasant. Who stole from his neighbours, set fire to their property, gave false witness at the court for a bottle of vodka? At the meetings of the *Zemstvo* and other local bodies, who was the first to fall foul of the peasants? A peasant.

Anton Chekhov, *The Russian Master and other stories*

[Chekhov] was very hospitable and loved it when people stayed to dinner, and he knew how to treat guests in his own peculiar way, simply and heartily. He would say, standing behind one's chair: "Listen, have some vodka. When I was young and healthy I loved it. I would pick mushrooms for a whole morning, get tired out, hardly able to reach home, and before lunch I would have two or three thimblefuls. Wonderful!"

Alexander Kuprin, *Reminiscences of Anton Chekhov*

The award for the highest number of times vodka occurs in the works of a Russian writer is easily won by Anton Chekhov. As a writer, he was realistic about the ever-present spirit in Russian life, but as a doctor he did not support over-indulgence in it. Of the great 19th-century Russian writers, he had perhaps the most balanced personality, and as a doctor he was sympathetic and generous.

His own life had been difficult. The son of a shopkeeper, he was born in Yalta in the south of Russia in 1860. Chekhov was left behind at sixteen to finish his schooling when his family escaped to Moscow to avoid their creditors. His father was a poor businessman, and when a drowned rat was found in a barrel of either oil or vodka in his store, he simply asked the priest to sprinkle the barrel with holy water to purify it. In any case, Chekhov eventually followed his family to Moscow where he trained as a doctor.

He made more money as a writer than from medicine, first dipping his pen in neat vodka when he was twenty-five. Several Moscow vodka companies were attacking each other's products in a series of notices in a Moscow newspaper. Chekhov responded in a satirical article that appeared in a magazine published in St. Petersburg called *Oskolki*, describing the vodka companies as "Satan's blood makers", a phrase that would recur in his fiction as "Satan's blood peddlers". The previous year, he had defined vodka as "a colourless drink that paints your nose red and blackens your reputation", a charge feared by Pyotr Smirnov who worried what such publicity would do to the reputation of his own company. Chekhov wrote:

> We have no news about the Afghan borders, but we have war in Moscow already… Englishmen are not waging war. Nor Russians. But Satan's blood makers – the tavern keepers and the vodka makers do it. *Casus belli* is a competition. Each enemy, trying to prove that his competitors' vodkas are no bloody good, sends torpedoes toward them and sinks them… Any means are used to pour pepper into the sleeping competitor's nose, to snooker him, and to hurt his reputation.

Smirnov probably never read the free advertisement for his famous "No.21" vodka that Chekhov awarded to him in a short story called *The Duel* in which a character is accused of corrupting small town inhabitants whom he:

> …taught to drink beer, which was also unknown here, and they are further indebted to him for an acquaintance with the various kinds of vodka, so that blindfolded they can distinguish Koshelev's vodka from Smirnov No.21.

Smirnov and Widow Popova, the two vodka makers that Chekhov had mentioned in his satirical attack, are amusingly transformed into the names of the two main characters of his farce, *The Bear*, which tells the story of how Elena Popova becomes a widow. Neither vodka company felt inclined to make use of the free publicity.

As Chekhov was having to support his entire family, which included two alcoholic brothers, his views on vodka were understandable. He wrote in a letter to one of those brothers that an aspect characterising cultured people was that they "do not swill vodka at all hours of the day and night".

Chekhov gave up drinking vodka in 1891 after a period of depression. As a realist writer, he could not avoid references to vodka in his fiction and plays, and as a doctor he would have treated alcoholic patients. His cruelly compassionate short story, *The Peasant*, is a full-scale attack on the destructiveness of vodka, but with a sensitive understanding of why the peasant could not function without it. Elsewhere he wrote that:

> The Russian is a great pig. If you ask him why he doesn't eat meat and fish, he justifies himself by the absence of transport, ways and communications, and so on, and yet vodka is to be found in the remotest villages and as much of it as you please. And yet one would have supposed that it would have been much easier to obtain meat and fish than vodka, which is more expensive and more difficult to transport.

Like Tolstoy, he did not allow his personal views to deny the peasants who worked for him their traditional New Year present of a barrel of vodka. A flag flown from his house, bought from the Moscow department store Muir and Mirrielees, let the peasants know that he was at home and was available to give them free treatment and medicine. They would be greeted by his two mongrel dogs, which were named after the department store's Scottish founders.

One of Chekhov's most amusing short stories is on the theme of temperance and sees the widow of an alcoholic hosting an annual celebration in his memory, including a meal where all intoxicating liquor is absent.

Having no illusions about his own health and the progression of his tuberculosis, Chekhov understood the significance of a glass of champagne he was given in bed by a doctor in Berlin. The writer's wife recorded that he drank a full glass before he remarked that he had not drunk champagne for a long time. He then turned on his side and died. His body was brought to Moscow by train in a refrigerated compartment normally used for oysters, a fact that somehow annoyed Gorky but would have amused Chekhov. He would probably not have been flattered that a brand of vodka would later be named after him and would be widely on sale as a "house" vodka in British pubs.

Anton Chekhov

III

Texts

Since vodka is as commonplace in Russia as tea is in the United Kingdom, most passages where vodka features in Russian fiction are not particularly memorable, although Gogol's passing references to the spirit are often amusing. Published last year, Andrei Gelasimov's *Thirst* is a moving novel about a Russian soldier who, burned beyond recognition in Chechnya, rarely leaves his apartment and spends most of his time drinking alone. With a refrigerator overflowing with vodka bottles, he is about to embark on a three-month drinking binge when a knock on the door and subsequent events change his perception of life.

Vodka, by Boris Starling, is set in the early days of the Russian Federation. Although the narrative centres around the privatisation of a vodka distillery, the attempts by Slav and Chechen mafia to control the vodka market through violence and murder contribute to a convincing portrayal of post-Soviet Russia and the economic signficance of vodka.

Entitled "Vodka", the eighth chapter of the third and final volume of Philip Pulman's *His Dark Materials* is well worth reading. For excellent period context, vodka and *samogon* feature in the detective novels of R.N. Morris, William Ryan and Martin Cruz Smith, with each covering different periods of Russian history.

Angel Pavement, by J. B. Priestley

The extract below from *Angel Pavement* by J. B. Priestley contains the first appearance of vodka in English fiction.

Miss Lilian Matfield is a typist for a wood-veneer business in Angel Pavement, London, and has boarded a docked ship to do some secretarial work for James Golspie, a new and fraudulent employee of the company. Golspie offers a drink to Miss Matfield from a bottle he has already opened:

He pointed to the tall bottle. "It'll warm you up. I'm going to have some. You join me." He poured out two small glasses of the colourless liquor.

"Shall I? What is it?"

"Vodka. It's the favourite tipple in these ships."

Vodka! She picked up the glass and put her nose to it. She had never tasted vodka before, never remembered ever having seen it before, but of course it was richly associated with her memories of romantic fiction of various kinds, and was tremendously thrilling, the final completing thrill of the afternoon's adventure. At once she could hear herself bringing the vodka into her account of the adventure at the Club. "And then, my dear," it would run, "I was given some vodka. There I was, in the cabin, swilling vodka like mad. Marvellous!"

"Come along, Miss Matfield," said Mr. Golspie, looking at her over his raised glass. "Down it goes. Happy days!" And he emptied his glass with one turn of the wrist.

"All right," she cried, raising hers. "What do I say? Cheerio?" Boldly she drained her glass, too, in one gulp. For a second or so, nothing happened but a curious aniseedy taste as the liquor slipped over her palate, but then, suddenly, it was as if an incendiary bomb had burst in her throat and sent white fire racing down every channel of her body. She gasped, laughed, coughed, all at once.

"That's the way, Miss Matfield. You put it down in great style. Try another. I'm going to have one. Just another for good luck." He filled the glasses again.

She floated easily now on a warm tide. It was very pleasant. She took the glass, hesitated, then looked up at him. "I'm not going to be tight, am I? If you make me drunk I shan't be able to type your letters, you know."

"Don't you worry about that," he told her, grinning amiably and then patting her shoulder. "You couldn't be soused on two glasses of this stuff, and you'll be as sober as a judge by the time you get back to Angel Pavement. It'll just make you feel warm and comfortable, and keep the cold out. Now then. Here she goes."

"Happy days!" cried Miss Matfield, smiling at him, and once more there came the aniseedy taste, the incendiary bomb, the racing white fire, and the final warm tide.

"Now I like you, Miss Matfield," he told her, with a full stare of approval.

"That was done in real style, like a good sport. You've got some character, not like most of these pink little ninnies of girls you see here. I noticed that right at the start. I said to myself, 'That girl's not only got looks but she's got character too.' I wish you were coming with us."

"Thank you."

"Well, it's a real compliment. Though I don't know that you'd like it. It'll be perishingly cold, and by tomorrow she'll be rolling like the devil all the way across the North Sea, and she'll start rolling again when we get into the Baltic. I know her of old. How d'you feel now?"

"Marvellous!" And she did. She rose and gathered her things together.

"Not too sober, though."

When they went out on to the upper deck, she stopped and looked down the river. Daylight had dwindled to a faint silver above and an occasional cold gleam on the water, and at any other time she would probably have been depressed or half frightened by the leaden swell of the river itself, the uncertain lights beyond, and the melancholy hooting, but now it all seemed wonderfully mysterious and romantic. For a minute or so, she lost herself in it. She was quite happy and yet she felt close to tears. It was probably the vodka.

"Sort of hypnotises you, doesn't it?" said Mr. Golspie gruffly, at her elbow.

"It does, doesn't it?" she said softly. At that moment, she decided that she liked Mr. Golspie and that he was an unusual and fascinating man. She also felt that she herself was fascinating, really rather wonderful.

The Marshal's Widow, by Anton Chekhov

The widow of an alcoholic invites various local dignitaries to a lunch in honour of her late husband:

The lunch is certainly exceptional. Everything that the flora and fauna of the country can furnish is on the table, but the only thing supernatural about it, perhaps, is that on the table there is everything except… alcoholic beverages. Lyubov Petrovna has taken a vow never to have in her house cards or spirituous liquors – the two sources of her husband's ruin. And the only bottles contain oil and vinegar, as though in mockery and chastisement of the guests who are to a man desperately fond of the bottle, and given to tippling.

"Please help yourselves, gentlemen!" the marshal's widow presses them. "Only you must excuse me, I have no vodka… I have none in the house."

The guests approach the table and hesitatingly attack the pie. But the progress with eating is slow. In the plying of forks, in the cutting up and munching, there is a certain sloth and apathy…

Evidently something is wanting.

"I feel as though I had lost something," one of the justices of the peace whispers to the other. "I feel as I did when my wife ran away with the engineer… I can't eat."

Marfutkin, before beginning to eat, fumbles for a long time in his pocket and looks for his handkerchief.

"Oh, my handkerchief must be in my greatcoat," he recalls in a loud voice, "and here I am looking for it," and he goes into the vestibule where the fur coats are hanging up.

He returns from the vestibule with glistening eyes, and at once attacks the pie with relish.

"I say, it's horrid munching away with a dry mouth, isn't it?" he whispers to Father Yevmeny. "Go into the vestibule, Father. There's a bottle there in my fur coat… Only mind you are careful; don't make a clatter with the bottle."

Father Yevmeny recollects that he has some direction to give to Luka, and trips off to the vestibule.

"Father, a couple of words in confidence," says Dvornyagin, overtaking him.

"You should see the fur coat I've bought myself, gentlemen," Hrumov boasts. "It's worth a thousand, and I gave – you won't believe it – two hundred and fifty! Not a farthing more."

At any other time the guests would have greeted this information with indifference, but now they display surprise and incredulity.

In the end they all troop out into the vestibule to look at the fur coat, and go on looking at it until the doctor's man Mikeshka carries five empty bottles out on the sly. When the steamed sturgeon is served, Marfutkin remembers that he has left his cigar case in his sledge and goes to the stable. That he may not be lonely on this expedition, he takes with him the deacon, who appropriately feels it necessary to have a look at his horse…

On the evening of the same day, Lyubov Petrovna is sitting in her study, writing a letter to an old friend in Petersburg:

"Today, as in past years," she writes among other things, "I had a memorial service for my dear husband. All my neighbours came to the service. They are a simple, rough set, but what hearts! I gave them a splendid lunch, but of course, as in previous years, without a drop of alcoholic liquor. Ever since he died from excessive drinking I have vowed to establish temperance in this district and thereby to expiate his sins. I have begun the campaign for temperance at my own house. Father Yevmeny is delighted with my efforts, and helps me both in word and deed. Oh, *ma chère*, if you knew how fond my bears are of me! The president of the *Zemstvo*, Marfutkin, kissed my hand after lunch, held it a long while to his lips, and, wagging his head in an absurd way, burst into tears: so much feeling but no words! Father Yevmeny, that delightful little old man, sat down by me, and looking tearfully at me kept babbling something like a child. I did not understand what he said, but I know how to understand true feeling. The police captain, the handsome man of whom I wrote to you, went down on his knees to me, tried to read me some verses of his own composition (he is a poet), but… his feelings were too much for him, he lurched and fell over… that huge giant went into hysterics, you can imagine my delight! The day did not pass without a hitch, however. Poor Alalykin, the president of the judges' assembly, a stout and apoplectic man, was overcome by illness and lay on the sofa in a state of unconsciousness for two hours. We had to pour water on him… I am thankful to Doctor Dvornyagin: he had brought a bottle of brandy from his dispensary and he moistened the patient's temples, which quickly revived him, and he was able to be moved…"

An Inadvertence, by Anton Chekhov

PYOTR PETROVITCH STRIZHIN, the nephew of Madame Ivanov, the colonel's widow – the man whose new goloshes were stolen last year – came home from a christening party at two o'clock in the morning. To avoid waking the household, he took off his things in the lobby, made his way on tiptoe to his room, holding his breath, and began getting ready for bed without lighting a candle.

Strizhin leads a sober and regular life. He has a sanctimonious expression of face, he reads nothing but religious and edifying books, but at the christening party, in his delight that Lyubov Spiridonovna had passed through her confinement successfully, he had permitted himself to drink four glasses of vodka and a glass of wine, the taste of which suggested something midway between vinegar and castor oil. Spirituous liquors are like seawater and glory: the more you imbibe of them, the greater your thirst. And now as he undressed, Strizhin was aware of an overwhelming craving for drink.

"I believe Dashenka has some vodka in the cupboard in the right-hand corner," he thought. "If I drink one wine-glassful, she won't notice it."

After some hesitation, overcoming his fears, Strizhin went to the cupboard. Cautiously opening the door he felt in the right-hand corner for a bottle and poured out a wine-glassful, put the bottle back in its place, then, making the sign of the cross, drank it off. And immediately something like a miracle took place. Strizhin was flung back from the cupboard to the chest with fearful force like a bomb. There were flashes before his eyes, he felt as though he could not breathe, and all over his body he had a sensation as though he had fallen into a marsh full of leeches. It seemed to him as though, instead of vodka, he had swallowed dynamite, which blew up his body, the house, and the whole street… His head, his arms, his legs – all seemed to be torn off and to be flying away somewhere to the devil, into space.

For some three minutes he lay on the chest, not moving and scarcely breathing, then he got up and asked himself: "Where am I?"

The first thing of which he was clearly conscious on coming to himself was the pronounced smell of paraffin.

"Holy saints," he thought in horror, "it's paraffin I have drunk instead of vodka."

The thought that he had poisoned himself threw him into a cold shiver, then into a fever. That it was really poison that he had taken was proved not only by the smell in the room but also by the burning taste in his mouth, the flashes before his eyes, the ringing in his head, and the colicky pain in his stomach. Feeling the approach of death and not buoying himself up with false hopes, he wanted to say goodbye to those nearest to him, and made his way to Dashenka's bedroom (being a widower, he had his sister-in-law called Dashenka, an old maid, living in the flat to keep house for him).

"Dashenka," he said in a tearful voice as he went into the bedroom, "dear Dashenka!"

Something grumbled in the darkness and uttered a deep sigh. "Dashenka."

"Eh? What?" A woman's voice articulated rapidly. "Is that you, Pyotr Petrovitch? Are you back already? Well, what is it? What has the baby been christened? Who was godmother?"

"The godmother was Natalya Andreyevna Velikosvyetsky, and the godfather Pavel Ivanitch Bezsonnitsin… I… I believe, Dashenka, I am dying. And the baby has been christened Olimpiada, in honour of their kind patroness… I… I have just drunk paraffin, Dashenka!"

"What next! You don't say they gave you paraffin there?"

"I must own I wanted to get a drink of vodka without asking you, and… and the Lord chastised me: by accident in the dark I took paraffin… What am I to do?"

Dashenka, hearing that the cupboard had been opened without her permission, grew more wide-awake… She quickly lighted a candle, jumped out of bed, and in her nightgown, a freckled, bony figure in curl-papers, padded with bare feet to the cupboard.

"Who said you could?" she asked sternly, as she scrutinized the inside of the cupboard. "Was the vodka put there for you?"

"I… I haven't drunk vodka but paraffin, Dashenka…" muttered Strizhin, mopping the cold sweat on his brow.

"And what did you want to touch the paraffin for? That's nothing to do with you, is it? Is it put there for you? Or do you suppose paraffin costs nothing? Eh? Do you know what paraffin is now? Do you know?"

"Dear Dashenka," moaned Strizhin, "it's a question of life and death, and you talk about money!"

"He's drunk himself tipsy and now he pokes his nose into the cupboard!" cried Dashenka, angrily slamming the cupboard door. "Oh, the monsters, the tormentors! I'm a martyr, a miserable woman, no peace day or night! Vipers, basilisks, accursed Herods, may you suffer the same in the world to come! I am going tomorrow! I am a maiden lady and I won't allow you to stand before me in your underclothes! How dare you look at me when I am not dressed!"

And she went on and on… Knowing that when Dashenka was enraged there was no moving her with prayers or vows or even by firing a cannon, Strizhin waved his hand in despair, dressed, and made up his mind to go to the doctor. But a doctor is only readily found when he is not wanted. After running through three streets and ringing five times at Dr. Tchepharyants', and seven times at Dr. Bultyhin's, Strizhin raced off to a chemist's shop, thinking possibly the chemist could help him. There, after a long interval, a little dark and curly-headed chemist came out to him in his dressing gown, with drowsy eyes, and such a wise and serious face that it was positively terrifying.

"What do you want?" he asked in a tone in which only very wise and dignified chemists of Jewish persuasion can speak.

"For God's sake… I entreat you…" said Strizhin breathlessly, "give me something. I have just accidentally drunk paraffin, I am dying!"

"I beg you not to excite yourself and to answer the questions I am about to put to you. The very fact that you are excited prevents me from understanding you. You have drunk paraffin. Yes?"

"Yes, paraffin! Please save me!"

The chemist went coolly and gravely to the desk, opened a book, became absorbed in reading it. After reading a couple of pages he shrugged one shoulder and then the other, made a contemptuous grimace and, after thinking for a minute, went into the adjoining room. The clock struck four, and when it pointed to ten minutes past the chemist came back with another book and again plunged into reading.

"H'm," he said as though puzzled, "the very fact that you feel unwell shows you ought to apply to a doctor, not a chemist."

"But I have been to the doctors already. I could not wake them up."

"H'm… you don't regard us chemists as human beings, and disturb our rest even at four o'clock at night, though every dog, every cat, can rest in peace… You don't try to understand anything, and to your thinking we are not people and our nerves are like cords."

Strizhin listened to the chemist, heaved a sigh, and went home.

"So I am fated to die," he thought.

And in his mouth was a burning and a taste of paraffin, there were twinges in his stomach, and a sound of boom, boom, boom in his ears. Every moment it seemed to him that his end was near, that his heart was no longer beating.

Returning home he made haste to write: "Let no one be blamed for my death," then he said his prayers, lay down and pulled the bedclothes over his head. He lay awake till morning expecting death, and all the time he kept fancying how his grave would be covered with fresh green grass and how the birds would twitter over it… And in the morning he was sitting on his bed, saying with a smile to Dashenka: "One who leads a steady and regular life, dear sister, is unaffected by any poison. Take me, for example. I have been on the verge of death. I was dying and in agony, yet now I am all right. There is only a burning in my mouth and a soreness in my throat, but I am all right all over, thank God… And why? It's because of my regular life."

"No, it's because it's inferior paraffin!" sighed Dashenka, thinking of the household expenses and gazing into space. "The man at the shop could not have given me the best quality, but that at three farthings. I am a martyr, I am a miserable woman. You monsters! May you suffer the same, in the world to come, accursed Herods…"

And she went on and on…

Notes From A Dead House, by F.M. Dostoevsky

Everywhere among the Russian people, a certain sympathy is felt for a drunken man; in prison he was positively treated with respect. There were certain aristocratic customs connected with prison revelry. The carousing convict always hired music. There was a little Pole in prison, a runaway soldier, a nasty little fellow who played the fiddle and had an instrument – his one possession in the world. He had no sort of trade, and his only way of earning money was by playing lively dances for convicts who were having a spree.

His duty was to follow his drunken employer from room to room and to play the fiddle with all his might. Often his face betrayed boredom and dejection. But the shout of 'Play on, you're paid to do it!' made him go on scraping away. The convict can always feel confident when he begins drinking that, if he gets too drunk, he will certainly be looked after, will be put in bed in time and hidden away if the authorities turn up, and all this will be quite disinterested. The sergeant and the veteran guards, who lived in the prison to keep discipline, could have their minds at rest too: the drunken convict could not create any disorder. All the prisoners in the room looked after him, and if he were noisy or unmanageable they would quickly restrain him and even tie him up. And so the inferior prison officials winked at drunkenness and were unwilling to notice it. They knew very well that if vodka were not allowed it would make things worse. But how was vodka obtained?

It was bought in the prison itself from the so-called 'publicans'. There were several of them, and they carried on their trade continuously and successfully, though the number of those who drank and 'made merry' was small, for merry-making costs money and the convicts' money is hard to earn. The publicans' operations were begun, managed and carried on in a very original way. Suppose a convict knows no trade and is not willing to exert himself (there were men like this), but is keen on getting money and of an impatient disposition, in a hurry to make his pile. If he has a little money to start with, he makes up his mind to trade in vodka: it's a bold and risky enterprise involving considerable danger. He may have to pay for it with a flogging, and lose his stock and his capital all at once.

But the publican takes the risk. He begins with a small sum, and so at first he smuggles the vodka into the prison himself, and, of course, disposes of it to great advantage. He repeats the experiment a second and a third time, and if he does not get caught he quickly sells his stock and only then builds up a real trade on a large scale: he becomes an entrepreneur, a capitalist, employs agents and assistants, runs far less risk and makes more and more money. His subordinates risk themselves for him.

There are always in the prison lots of men who have wasted all they have on cards or drink, wretched ragged creatures who have no trade but have a certain pluck and daring. The only asset such a man has left is his back; it may still be of some use to him and so the spendthrift profligate decides to turn it to profit. He goes to the publican and offers his services for smuggling vodka; a well-to-do publican has several such working for him. Somewhere outside the prison there is some person – a soldier, a workman, sometimes even a woman – who for a comparatively large commission buys vodka at a tavern with the publican's money and conceals it in some out-of-the-way place where the convicts go to work. Almost always the intermediary tests the quality of the vodka to begin with, and ruthlessly fills up the measure with water; the publican may take it or leave it – a convict is not in a position to make his own terms. He must be thankful that he has got the vodka, however poor the quality, and has not lost his money altogether.

The publican introduces his agents to the intermediary beforehand, and then they go to the latter carrying with them the guts of a bullock, which have been washed and then filled with water to keep them supple and fit to hold vodka. When he has filled the guts with vodka the convict winds them round himself where they will be least conspicuous. I need not say that this calls forth all the ingenuity, all the thievish cunning of the smuggler. His honour is to some extent involved: he has to deceive both the guards and the sentries. He does deceive them: the guard, often a raw recruit, is never a match for a clever thief. Of course the guard is the subject of special study beforehand; besides, the time and place where he is working is all carefully considered, too, by the smuggler. The convict may be building a stove; he climbs on to the stove; who can tell what he is doing there? A guard cannot be expected to climb after him. On his way to the prison he takes some money in his hand, fifteen or twenty silver kopeks, in case of need, and waits for the corporal at the gate. The corporal examines every convict returning from work, and feels him over before opening the prison door to him. The man smuggling in vodka usually reckons on the corporal's scrupling to handle him too minutely in some parts. But sometimes the wily corporal does not stand on ceremony and discovers the vodka. Then there is only one thing left to do: the smuggler, unseen by the guard, silently slips into the corporal's hand the coin he has been keeping concealed in his own. It sometimes happens that, thanks to this manoeuvre, he gets successfully into the prison with the vodka.

But sometimes this method does not answer, and then he has to pay with his last asset, his back. It is reported to the major, the asset is flogged, and cruelly flogged; the vodka is confiscated and the agent takes it all on himself without giving away his employer, and, be it noted, not because he scorns to tell tales, but simply because it does not pay him to do so. He would be flogged anyway; his only consolation would be that the other man would be flogged too. But he will need his employer again, though in accordance with custom and previous agreement the smuggler gets nothing from his employer to compensate him for the flogging. As for telling tales in general, it is very common. In prison the man who turns traitor is not exposed to humiliation; indignation against him is unthinkable. He is not shunned, the others make friends with him; in fact, if you were to try and point out the loathsomeness of treachery, you would not be understood. The convict with whom I had broken off all relations, a mean and depraved creature who had been a gentleman, was friendly with the major's orderly, Fedka, and served him as a spy, while the latter reported all he heard about the convicts to the major. Every one of us knew this, yet no one ever dreamed of punishing the scoundrel or even reproaching him for it.

But I am wandering from my subject. It happens, of course, that vodka is smuggled in successfully. Then the publican takes the guts, pays for them, and begins to count the cost. It turns out when he reckons it that the stuff has cost him a great deal, and so to increase his profit he dilutes the vodka once more, adding almost an equal bulk of water, and then he is ready for his customers. On the first holiday, sometimes even on a working day, the customer turns up: this is a convict who has been working like an ox for some months, and has saved up his money in order to spend it all on drink on some day fixed beforehand. Long before it arrives, this day has been the object of the poor toiler's dreams at night and happy day-dreams over his work, and its fascination has kept up his spirits through the weary routine of prison life. At last the happy day dawns in the east; his money has been saved, not taken away, not stolen, and he brings it to the publican. To begin with, the latter gives him the vodka as pure as possible, that is, only twice diluted; but as the bottle gets emptier he invariably fills it up again with water. A cup of vodka costs five or six times as much as in a tavern. You can imagine how many cups of such vodka must be drunk, and what they will have cost before the point of intoxication is reached. But from having lost the habit of drinking, and having abstained from it so long, the convict readily gets drunk and he usually goes on drinking till he has spent all his money. Then he brings out all his new clothes; the publican is a pawnbroker as well. He first gets hold of the newly acquired personal possessions, then the old things and finally the prison clothes. When he has drunk up everything to the last rag, the drunken convict lies down to sleep, and next day, waking up with the inevitable splitting headache, he vainly entreats the publican to give him just a sip of vodka as a pick-me-up. Mournfully he endures his sad plight and the same day sets to work again, and works again for several months unceasingly, dreaming of the happy day of debauch lost and gone forever, and by degrees beginning to take heart again and look forward to another similar day, still far away, but sure to come sometime in its turn.

As for the publican, after making a huge sum of money – some dozens of roubles – he gets the vodka ready for the last time, adding no water to it, for he means it for himself – he has done enough of trading, it is time for him to enjoy himself too! Then begins an orgy of drinking, eating and music. With such means at his disposal he even softens the hearts of the inferior prison officials. The debauch sometimes lasts several days. All the vodka he has prepared is soon drunk, of course; then the prodigal resorts to the other publicans, who are on the lookout for him, and drinks until he has spent every farthing! However carefully the convicts guard their drunken fellow, he is sometimes seen by a higher official, by the major or the officer on duty. He is taken to the guard-house, stripped of his money if he has it on him and finally flogged. He shakes himself, goes back into the prison, and a few days later takes up his trade in vodka again.

Russian peasants 1823

IV

Vodka and Music

As we have seen, the Polish writer and artist Witkacy had suggested in his book on narcotics that only writers and artists who were certain that they could write nothing of value without alcohol should be allowed it to excess in order to fuel their talent until they were burnt out, their brilliant legacy already secured.

Other excuses rooted in the country's autocratic political system were found to justify excessive drinking by Russia's creative classes. It was said that the disappointment over the reforms of Alexander II in the 1860s fomented an upsurge of vodka drinking by:

> …the more sensitive, more responsive writers in society [who] saw that the freedom they had imagined was not at all what they got in reality, that individuality was still enslaved …in Mother Russia along with the most shameless, most vile brute force. And these wise men, the salt of the Russian earth, all of them young and life-loving, were driven to drink from the goblet of green wine.

Although this seems like a flimsy rationale to excuse excessive vodka drinking by "the sensitive", the limitations of the reforms had in fact encouraged writers and composers to drink vast amounts of vodka. It was the only protest of extreme behaviour against the establishment that would not attract the attention of the secret police constantly on the lookout for subversion. "An intense worship of Bacchus was considered to be almost obligatory for a writer of that period," a contemporary reflected, and another remarked that, "Talented people in Russia who love the simple folk cannot but drink."

There seems to be some truth in the notion that vodka was indeed a creative catalyst, probably because the purity of the spirit meant that any creative boost was not proceeded by a hangover that would debilitate the drinker. The Leningrad-born poet Lev Loseff, who emigrated to America and became Joseph Brodsky's biographer, stated he owed:

> …everything good in my life to vodka. Vodka was the catalyst of spiritual emancipation, opening doors into interesting cellars of the subconscious and at the same time teaching me not to be afraid of people or the authorities.

From the testimonies of some Russian composers, vodka appears to have been a positive force in their lives and essential to their music, although the word "vodka" was often used by critics as a term of abuse to describe composers' work. When Rachmaninoff's Fourth Piano Concerto was first performed, an American critic wrote that, "Mme. Cécile Chaminade might safely have perpetrated it on her third glass of vodka."

The Witkacy theory applied to Modest Mussorgsky who died at the age of 42 in 1881, although it was a fatal brandy that actually killed him rather than vodka, which he drank to excess all his life. He and other creative rebels frequented low taverns in St. Petersburg as a gesture of solidarity towards the peasants and to distance themselves from the more reputable artistic circles of the city.

Mussorgsky composed in the Maly Yaroslavets, a respectable restaurant where he had a private room with a ready vodka supply to hand. (The place would later attract Chekhov and other writers partly because of its reputation for being the watering hole of choice for bohemian drinkers.) Mussorgsky had extraordinarily original musical gifts, but while his fondness for vodka prevented his completing some works, it did not mar the quality of what he actually wrote. His doctor, who had tried to help the composer to moderate his vodka intake, left details of a faultless concert performance given by Mussorgsky as a piano accompanist when he was extremely drunk. The doctor observed Mussorgsky in his room at the Maly Yaroslavet:

> On the dirty table stood some vodka and some scraps of miserable food. In saying goodbye to me he got up with difficulty, but saw me to the door and bowed me out in a manner which, though not quite worthy of Louis XIV, was quite amazing for someone so completely tight…

Mussorgsky arrived on time at the venue where his concert was to take place, and while he was waiting he proceeded to polish off all the drinks that he could find. He astonished everyone with his brilliant pianism, playing the music at first sight and in different keys to those in which it was written so as to suit the singer's voice.

Tchaikovsky, who drank vodka nearly every day, wrote a song about a fool who drinks vodka in the tsar's tavern It was the only song of the set it appeared in that did not have a dedication. It might well have been dedicated to himself. The normally discreet Rimsky-Korsakov recalled that Tchaikovsky drank copiously, and very few could keep up with him whilst simultaneously retaining their mental and physical powers in the way that he could.

For Tchaikovsky, hardly a day passed without vodka, and when he tried to give it up, his resolve broke after a short period of abstinence. The composer made frequent references to the spirit in letters and in his diary, noting in the latter that he could hardly hold a pen because he was as drunk as a sailor.

Tchaikovsky's longest commentary on vodka came in a furious response to what he considered a sanctimonious anti-vodka account by a Russian anthropologist. Apart from throwing light on the normally intensely secretive composer, what he called "the first stage of drunkennness" may also help to explain the contribution made by vodka to creativity that others also experienced:

> It is said that to abuse oneself with alcoholic drink is harmful.

> I readily agree with that. But nevertheless, I, that is, a sick person, full of "neuroses", absolutely cannot do without the alcoholic "poison" against which Mr Miklukho-Maklai protests. A person with such a strange name is extremely happy that he does not know the delights of vodka and other alcoholic drinks. But how unjust it is to judge others by yourself and to prohibit to others that which you yourself do not like. Now I, for example, am drunk every night, and cannot do without it… In the first stage of drunkenness, I feel complete happiness and understand, in such a condition, infinitely more than I do when I am without the Miklukho-Maklai poison!!!

When Tchaikovsky's drinking was controlled and did not go beyond the "first stage of drunkenness", he seemed to enter a state of mind, which it can be assumed was conducive to his composing. In the 20th century, nearly all of the noted Russian composers drank vodka including those who ended up living in different countries because of the 1917 revolution. Prokofiev, who was unusual for being allowed to leave Russia with the blessing of the Soviet Union, is one of the few Russian composers who drank very little, and although he had no need to be cautious, he preferred jokes and good humour to the vodka-inspired soul-searching of Tchaikovsky and Shostakovich.

Stravinsky, who was exiled after the events of 1917, settled in America and drank vodka in copious amounts. Born in St. Petersburg where he studied music, Stravinsky often enjoyed vodka and *zakuski* with his teacher, Nikolai Rimsky-Korsakov, whose name, an American critic of his *Scheherazade* declared, suggested "fierce whiskers stained with vodka". The friendship with Stravinsky was not shared by the older composer's son, Andrei, who dismissed Stravinsky's *Petrushka* as "Russian vodka with French perfumes".

Supremely careful with his money, Stravinsky bought a vodka distillery in Ukraine when he was living in Paris just before the First World War. It would have been an extremely good investment if history had not decided otherwise. He made vodka memorable in his

The Soldier's Tale, using a modified plot from a Russian folk tale in which in Stravinsky's words:

> The soldier tricks the Devil into drinking too much vodka. He then gives the Devil a handful of shot to eat, assuring him that it's caviar, and the Devil greedily swallows it and dies.

Stravinsky was frequently drunk on vodka. While directing a recording session of his *Ebony Concerto*, he told the jazz pianist Jimmy Rowles that he was using the wrong fingering and asked in the same breath if he could have some vodka. One of the trumpeters dashed off across the street, returning "with a great big glass of vodka. And Stravinsky knocked that mother off like a real Russian".

Living to the age of 88, Stravinsky's vodka intake caused him no obvious harm, but Shostakovich, who remained in the Soviet Union for all of his life, was in a constant state of nerves like Tchaikovsky. Punctilious about toasting friends with vodka, Shostakovich asked a friend in Tashkent to drink a glass of vodka at the same time as he would in Moscow in memory of a musician who had died. By the time the composer was 65, he was advised to give up on the spirit after a heart attack in 1971. Two years later Shostakovich defied his doctor and had a glass of vodka when visited by a friend. To the composer's amazement, the vodka somehow banished a "writer's block" of two years standing during which he had been unable to write down a single musical note. The following day Shostakovich began work on his Fourteenth Quartet, which he completed in a month, leaving him in no doubt that the vodka was responsible for the renewal of his creative powers.

Although it cannot be stated with certainty that vodka contains a mysterious ingredient that contributes to creativity, it is certain that without the spirit – whether it was drunk in Imperial or Soviet Russia or beyond – the music of the great Russian composers would have been very different.

Appendix

Early Morning at the Tavern by Leonid Solomatkin

Last Tavern at the City Gates by Vasily Perov

How Smirnov became Smirnoff: A History of a Vodka Dynasty

> In 1886 Pierre Smirnoff produced a vodka so exquisite, he shared it with his closest friends. The Czar of Russia, the King of Spain, the King of Sweden…
>
> It was Pierre Smirnoff's artistry, not his family tree, that endeared him to Tsar Alexander III back in 1886. It was then, with just one taste of Pierre Smirnoff's vodka, that the Czar appointed him the purveyor of spirits to the Russian Imperial Court.
>
> After that, Pierre Smirnoff enjoyed an ever expanding circle of friends. Both Russian and European nobility immediately recognised the unique taste of his creation for what it was. Highly superior vodka. Naturally. Because he created it with only superior ingredients, in the finest Russian tradition. Today, the tradition continues. The unique taste which captivated 19th century aristocracy is available to you. It's called Smirnoff de Czar. And one sip will tell you why this very special reserve vodka is meant to be shared with only your closest friends.

A large dose of creative licence characterises the 1982 advertisement for American-produced Smirnoff vodka, for the founder of the Moscow Smirnov Vodka Company, Pyotr Arsenijevic Smirnov, had never been friendly with the tsar of Russia any more than Gustav Fabergé when he was appointed "Goldsmith by special appointment to the Imperial Crown". Smirnov would have been delighted to have achieved such an enormous social promotion alongside his appointment as a vodka "Purveyor to His Imperial Majesty's Court"; he would have been even more surprised at the transformation of his Russian name to the French "Pierre Smirnoff".

Whether trading as Smirnoff in Europe and America in the 20th century or as Smirnov in Imperial Russia in the previous century, the company appeared to be an extraordinarily resilient survivor. It had not always been so.

Smirnov was born in 1831 in Yaroslavl, about one hundred and sixty miles from Moscow. As the son of a serf, he had no experience of life beyond the landed estate to which his family was tied. That someone from the humblest of backgrounds could create one of the largest vodka companies in Russia was extraordinary enough, but if anyone could have foreseen that from its ghostly vodka vapours would materialise in America and Europe the most famous name in spirits a century after its founder's birth, this would have seemed like the ramblings of a drunken dreamer.

Smirnov's rise to the summit of the distilling world in Imperial Russia was accomplished by hard work, advertising flair, greed, snobbery and sycophancy. These characteristics proved to be vital, for his family did not have any kind of aristocratic ties that they could use for financial or social leverage. They were former serfs who had bought their freedom in stages before it was granted in full by law in 1863.

Smirnov had managed to secure an exit visa from the landowner of his village in 1846 when he was fifteen, allowing him to find work away from the landowner's estate. He walked the entire journey from his Yaroslavl home to Moscow where he was taken on by Ivan Smirnov, a younger brother of his father, who managed a wine cellar in a poor area of the city.

Ivan came to own the business outright when his employer died, and transformed the wine shop into a company that also sold illegal vodka. The shabby premises above the shop where the Smirnov family lived belonged to the church which lay just a few yards away. The church was unlawfully situated, as it was forbidden for church entrances to be closer than 280 feet from premises dealing in alcohol. The generous contributions Ivan made to the church funds doubtless closed a few clerical mouths, allowing others to open for vodka.

The semi-literate Smirnovs seemed born to run businesses. While Ivan expanded his wine shop, Pyotr's father came to Moscow in 1858 where he set up his own wine cellar with help from his son. It could hardly have been a better time to start a business, for the emancipation of the serfs was only one of the tsar's reforms. All the restrictions on distilling vodka were abolished along with the tax-farming system. The whole processing of vodka, from harvesting grain to selling the finished spirit, was open to anyone. Moscow now welcomed merchants along with other new freedoms in the most significant period of westernisation since Peter the Great's rule. (Alexander II was later blown to pieces in 1881 by a bomb tossed into his carriage, ironically when he was just about to sign an order granting further freedoms.)

One of the best features of the changed system was the reduction in the price of vodka by sixty-five percent from twenty-five roubles per bucket to eight roubles and sixty kopeks. But it resulted in the conversion of every grimy cellar in Moscow into a tavern. However dingy or unsanitary, all had to be supplied with vodka, and with this in mind, Pyotr Smirnov took over a ramshackle building with a still and a steam boiler already installed. Nevertheless, he did not distil the alcohol base but imported it, experimenting with the infusion of various herbs and fruits. It was said that Smirnov had been given a winning lottery ticket by a female friend, which financed the vodka factory. When she demanded to have the ticket back, he refused.

The vodka reform was not wasted on Ivan Smirnov, who also enlarged his now-legal vodka operations in 1865. His distilling efforts have been largely forgotten, eclipsed by the success of his nephew Pyotr. But although the vodka king achieved a great deal on his own initiative, he owed some of his success to his uncle, who had expanded his factories and retail outlets with great acumen.

The two men became business rivals, but while Ivan was content with the awards his vodka brought him from trade exhibitions, the younger man, obsessed with rising in society, would stop at nothing to promote his own vodka. The artistic style of Ivan's publicity and advertisements for his products showed an awareness of contemporary art. They had none of the formal designs chosen by Pyotr Smirnov that pandered to the upper strata of society to which he longed to be admitted.

If family legend is correct, Ivan was responsible for creating a pure, clear vodka in his "illegal" days as early as 1815. A new method of filtering spirits through charcoal – the greatest single achievement so far in advancing the purity of vodka – had been discovered around 1785. As the charcoal-filtering method had been widely publicised, it seems unlikely that Pyotr Smirnov was the first vodka producer to take it up as he later claimed, and the method was probably the secret behind his uncle Ivan's own pure vodka.

The method was discovered by a German scientist, Johann Tobias Lowitz, in St. Petersburg. As a boy, Lowitz saw his father impaled by a rebel tsarist pretender, and he himself was "afflicted by tape worm and deprived during the last years of the use of his left hand in consequence of the fall of the glass-covering of his mineral cabinet, which had cut the tendons and nerves of his forearm, his life becoming irksome and disagreeable."

These handicaps did not stop Lowitz, whose discovery was tailor-made for improving vodka:

> By merely shaking corn-based spirit with powdered charcoal, fusel oils and unpleasant esters [impurities] could be removed, improving the liquor's aroma and taste; any undesirable colour would be quickly whisked away, producing a crystal-clear product.

Uncle Ivan aside, Pyotr had many other established competitors of whom the widow Popova was the most famous. Her vodka was well-known for being triple distilled and was consequently acclaimed to be extra pure. Popova and other distillers supplied the Imperial Court with their products, but they too would be swept away by the 1917 revolution. A relative newcomer, Smirnov's vodka was no better than any of his rivals', especially as he did not distil his own spirit. How then did Smirnov manage to beat all of his competitors to become the most famous vodka producer in Russia? The answer lay in his gift for marketing. He excelled at promotion and his abilities put him in a different league to his rivals.

An example of Smirnov's imaginative flair for publicity came when he went to the Khitrov market in Moscow, a favourite spot for those looking for casual work. Carefully avoiding anyone who was not sober, he enlisted about fifteen men. He took them back to his house, fed them and gave each man three roubles. They were told to go back to where they lived – which represented a wide area of Moscow – to order meat soups in their local tavern and demand Smirnov vodka. They were to refuse any other brand if Smirnov was not available and complain that the tavern was at fault for not stocking "the most remarkable vodka there is".

The men were to repeat their performance in the next bar, and it was said Smirnov was overwhelmed that evening with orders from "people demanding ten, fifteen, or twenty boxes of vodka. The vodka gushed out across Moscow." The men were then asked to travel further afield by rail, and their demand for Smirnov vodka "travelled like a virus, infecting one town after another". Selling vodka on a large scale was lucrative. Within ten years, Smirnov employed sixty workers and produced one hundred thousands buckets of drinks including vodka.

He moved to larger premises close to the Kremlin, but the narrow streets that led to it were constantly jammed with cartloads of goods, impeding the quick delivery of the perishable fresh fruit Smirnov needed for his vodkas and contributing to the congestion in the area. While not quite resorting to bribery, Smirnov managed to invoke the help of the police to clear the streets. It was a good example of Smirnov's refusal to be defeated by problems obstructing his ultimate ambition of supplying the Imperial Court with his vodka and other products including wine and liqueurs.

But the seal of the Imperial Court's approval was a distinction that required qualifications beyond evidence of a satisfactory product. Smirnov's first application to the office of the tsar in 1869 was a failure. The refusal drove Smirnov to reconsider his tactics. As far as his business was concerned, he would take part in international trade exhibitions and expand the sale of his vodka beyond Moscow over the next decade and a half. Smirnov took great care to target his charitable donations to the causes which would garner the most attention for him from high society. A large donation to the Moscow Committee of Beggars was rewarded with a medal and a ribbon, which could be worn on suitable occasions. As a member of the committee, Smirnov was automatically granted the title of titular consul. This came ninth out of the fourteen ranks of the civil service – a system established by Peter the Great and made familiar to west Europeans by Russian fiction.

For Smirnov, the entitlement to wear the formal uniform of his rank was an advertisement of his achievement and position. He was already a merchant of the second guild in Moscow. Although it was an honourable position and limited in membership, membership of the first guild in Moscow opened doors in Moscow society that the second guild could not. Additionally, a fine uniform with a sword as well as an entitlement to use a carriage pulled by two horses instead of a cart and one horse, were social distinctions denied to the second-guild merchants. Moreover, after twelve years of membership, merchants' children could be educated at schools attended by the aristocracy.

Smirnov was granted his first-guild licence in 1871, for which he paid an annual fee of about £4,500 at present-day prices. However, the social benefits and additional trading rights conferred by membership were incalculable and another step towards achieving the approval of the Imperial Court.

Smirnov confidently petitioned Tsar Alexander III with a suitably sycophantic letter in 1885, which summarised his achievements:

> For many years, I have been trading foreign and Russian wines in Moscow. My wine is consumed in all corners of the Russian

> Empire and is even sold abroad. With tireless personal labour, I have grown my business to the widest of proportions. I pay to the state treasury, in the form of excise taxes and customs duties, more than 2.5 million roubles per year. I was honoured to receive the highest awards for the quality of my wine – two State Coats of Arms from the Philadelphia International Exhibition of 1876 and from the Russian Exhibition of 1882. It is my wish to attain the greatest of joys – to become the Purveyor of wines and vodkas to the Court of His Majesty…

Signs of recognition came from St. Petersburg when Smirnov was asked to supply the Imperial Court there with his products. He quickly followed the request with a second letter even more gushing than the first.

Smirnov waited two anxious years for an answer to this appeal. At last, the eighteen years of gifting large sums to charities, earning medals at trade fair exhibitions and doing nothing disreputable to attract unwelcome attention finally paid off. A letter arrived in 1886 in which the Emperor deigned "Pyotr Smirnov to be named purveyor of the Highest Court with the right to carry the State emblem on his signboards. This highest honour is reported to the Head of the Court department in Moscow."

For a serf who was scarcely literate and who had received little practical help beyond the lottery ticket, Smirnov's achievement was remarkable. His vodka, drunk by the lowest peasant, would now also be served in the Imperial palaces. It is not hard to imagine the vodka master's delight when he received the news that his ultimate ambition in life had been achieved. The following day, Smirnov announced in the newspapers that he was changing his labels to include the Imperial double eagle and suitable wording that would reflect his appointment. He proudly ended his notice with the words, "Purveyor of His Imperial Majesty's Court, Pyotr Smirnov."

The announcement may have caused the other vodka producers some amusement, for Smirnov was not the only supplier of vodka to the Imperial palaces. Furthermore, the appointment was not to the court of the tsar, but to the lesser St. Petersburg court of a younger brother of Alexander III, the Grand Duke Sergei Alexandrovich. However, by way of careful wording, Smirnov always implied he had been granted the superior appointment, and when the Grand Duke was assassinated in 1905, the warrant displayed on Smirnov products should have been removed.

The royal appointment came just as there were signs that the regulations surrounding the vodka industry, which had proved to be so beneficial to Smirnov and other producers, was coming to an end. Alexander III wanted the whole alcohol industry in Russia to be examined in order to discover what positive changes could be made to reduce the endless surge of drunkenness set in train by the 1863 reforms.

The proposed changes included standardising the strength of vodka as well as stating what exactly vodka as a substance was by law and what items could be sold in taverns. More worrying was the threatened reintroduction of a state monopoly. All of these modifications would mean that Smirnov would no longer have control of his empire. Other factors threatened the stability of the established vodka industry. The temperance movement, supported by Tolstoy amongst others, was becoming increasingly noisy. The young Chekhov accused Smirnov in a newspaper of peddling "Satan's Blood", sneering at him for taking part in a vodka war in which distillers attacked each other in the press. Worse was to follow.

In preparation for the standardising of vodka as well as the labelling of the actual spirit as "vodka" instead of "bread wine" and other assorted names, the Imperial Chemical Laboratory analysed Smirnov's and other distillers' vodka. As Smirnov refused to divulge his "secret recipe", the analysts' task of comparing the vodkas from the private distillers was made harder. But the laboratory still worked out that Smirnov's vodka contained the greatest amount of ethyl acetate – an irritant to the nose, throat and eyes – of all the vodkas it examined. The report stated that:

According to the results of the analysis into the production

> process, it would be difficult to find that P. A. Smirnov's table wine [vodka] was the best, though it is still extremely popular... This finding demonstrates that the product's reputation doesn't always depend on the quality. Obviously a very considerable role here belongs to the way a factory distributes its products and on the talent to make a product's appearance more attractive. Very often, the product's reputation depends on its harmonious name, bottle shape, colourful label, or just the price of the product.

The report found that there was no real difference between the composition of the most expensive vodka on offer and the cheapest Smirnov vodka enjoyed by the undiscerning drunks who haunted the Khitrov market. Although Smirnov made an effort to change his purification methods, the real trouble stemmed from the fact that he did not distil the spirit himself but bought in low-grade vodka from Estonia before purifying it in Moscow. But, as the report accurately summarised, Smirnov's marketing drive concentrated on presentation of the product rather than the quality of the product itself. Despite the laboratory report, Smirnov had made a great contribution to raising the profile of vodka, and nobody was ever poisoned by it.

Smirnov died in 1898, and the company. struggling due to the changes brought about by the state monopoly, was reduced to bankruptcy by the incompetent management of the vodka king's sons.

Perhaps remembering the whimsical bear-shaped bottles once used to suggest the strength of Smirnov vodka, the sons mounted one last campaign. At a trade fair in Nizhniy Novgorod, wanting to demonstrate that they were still owners of a flourishing enterprise, the sons erected a stage in the main pavilion, which was grand and luxurious. They hired bears to walk, dance, bow and parade around a large stage as well as bring drinks to the audience. This unprecedented spectacle, with its free refreshments to boot, attracted a huge number of people. Vladimir, the third eldest of the Smirnov brothers, would later recall, "The crowd was dense. It was hard to move through it. Everyone wanted to toast with the bear."

According to Vladimir, all but two of the bears were either people in bear costumes or clockwork animals. But there were two real bears, held tightly by a leash, which were:

> fed so much vodka that they could not stand. First, they lowered themselves onto all four paws, then sat down and then finally fell asleep. Bears are big lovers of vodka. You did not need to ask them to drink it. They drank willingly, holding the bottle in their front paws.

The Smirnovs later published advertisements featuring bears holding Smirnov bottles, but the promotion did little to prop up the sagging company.

When the Russian Revolution took place, Vladimir, a playboy and racing addict, fled the country with his wife. After a tortuous journey to find refuge, the couple eventually settled in Lviv in Poland, part of present-day Ukraine, after a short stay in Istanbul.

When Vladimir lived in Moscow, he had little interest in vodka beyond the money it supplied, and he sold his share and all of his rights in the company to his elder brother. His family connection was now his only financial asset, as he was virtually penniless. In 1924, he managed to sell a licence to a local vodka producer in Lviv to make Smirnoff (he had changed his surname in an effort to feel more European). He tried to recreate the famous No.21 from memory and sent to Moscow for an old 1912 Smirnov catalogue, which he used to copy the label design. But as he admitted in his memoirs, No.21 did not resemble the Moscow vodka, for the method of distillation was totally different, as was the water supply. This was finally proved when the famous Smirnoff 21, on sale in the UK and America, was analysed and compared to the original recipe that had survived in Moscow.

Ultimately, the Smirnoff name would forever be associated with vodka because of Pyotr's efforts to make his vodka stand out, for the reproductions of the prize-winning medallion awards and the display of the Imperial Russian coat of arms were more than mere decoration. They were essential to sell the vodka made by Vladimir Smirnoff and would prove to be an indispensable part of the package when he sold off all of his rights in 1933 to an American-Russian émigré, the enterprising Rudolph Kunett whose family had supplied the pre-purified vodka to Smirnov in Moscow.

The Smirnov vodka of Imperial Russia survived the turbulence of the Russian Revolution before it was reinvented to become the Smirnoff of today. Like its imperial predecessor, Smirnoff became a market leader, but the actual taste of the vodka changed completely during its travels from Russia to Europe and America before its return trip to the East.

Pyotr Arsenijevic Smirnov

Spoilt for choice in Warsaw

Notes

Introduction

"[Miss Matfield] …had never tasted vodka before…": J. B. Priestley, *Angel Pavement* p 259
"failing to get the reckless Russian spirit he wanted…": Henry J.Wood, *My Life of Music* p 268
"his passion for roast beef and port wine…": Ivan Turgenev, *House of Gentlefolk* p 6
"Nobody in the world knows what vodka is…": Will Rogers, *There's Not a Bathing Suit in Russia and Other Bare Facts* p 14
The Russian Story
"Among all the Slavonic nations…: J.G. Kohl, *Russia and the Russians in 1842* p 130
"*Kabak* in the Russian language signifies a public house…": J. G. Georgi, *Russia or, a compleat historical account* p115
"Precious *votki*, the nectar of the Russian peasants…": Robert Lyall, *The Character Of The Russians* p 371
"Events of a… festive character are celebrated…": John Murray, *Handbook for Travellers in Russia, Poland and Finland* pp 29, 31, 40
"great drunkards and take a great pride…": quoted in White, *Russia goes Dry* p 5
"is sold *aqua-vitae…*": Giles Fletcher, *Of the Russe Commonwealth*, London,1591, cited in Berry & Crummey (eds), *Rude and Barbarous Kingdom* p 168
"came with their husbands to a carouse…": and subsequent quotations Samuel H. Baron, (ed.), *The Travels of Olearius in*

Seventeenth-Century Russia pp142–146
"not to drive drunkards away…": Pokhlebkin, *A History of Vodka* p49
"a singular attempt to jump out…": quoted in Nicholas Riasanovskyk, *The Image of Peter the Great in Russian History and Thought* p234
"a mediocre, if not savage, mind…": Aleksander Solzhenitsyn, quoted in *Pushkin's Children* p161
"used to refresh himself with his favourite beverage of vodka spiced with cayenne pepper…": Christopher Marsden, *Palmyra of the North* p52
"There is an appalling situation…" *Black Enterprise* Magazine, USA, October 1991 p137
"Presently came several evil apostles…": quoted in M. N. Pokrovsky, *History Of Russia,* p320
"Who is to be Permitted to Possess Vats…" Elizaveta Petrovna Romanova, quoted in Pokhlebkin, *A History of Vodka* p131
"1,200 litres of mash, containing 340 litres of grain": Pokhlebkin, *A History of Vodka* p158
"*Anisovaya* (aniseed), *Beryosovaya...*" found on website: www.eng.kristall.ru/
"to eat of the sweet and the savoury…": Leitch Ritchie, *Russia and the Russians* p86
"This drink has a magical power…": quoted in Ian Wisniewski, *Vodka* p26
"The wife herself in days of yore…": Yurii Ovsiannikov, *Lubok* illust. 45

Russian Daily Life in Vodka

"the signal for general mirth…": Robert Lyall, *The Character of the Russians and a detailed history of Moscow* p401
"in general it was doled out…": *Leitch Ritchie, Russia And The Russians* p139
"The profit to the farmer retailer was as much as 100,000…": Smith & Christian, *Bread and Salt* p304

"No other major source of revenue…": Smith & Christian, *Bread and Salt* p305
"It was the state's thirst for revenue…": Smith & Christian, *Bread and Salt* p301
"the vodka industry was…": Duane A. Baur, *Russia's Vodka and Russia* p 3 in a paper for TCC Humanities, Saint Petersburg
"…of all the traits I discovered in the Russian people…": John Ross Browne, *The Land Of Thor*, p74
"Damn na vodku…", Murray's Handbook for Travellers in Russia, Poland and Finland, p31
"…bilge-water, vitriol, turpentine…": G.A. Sala, *A Journey Due North in the Summer of 1856*, p61
"we drink the damned vodka at weddings…": quoted in Kate Transchel, *Under the Influence* p15
"more civilised forms of entertainment…": Transchel, *Under the Influence* p15
"Everyone drinks – the young…", and subsequent quotations: Smith & Christian, *Bread and Salt* p310
"*pomoch* is inconceivable without vodka": quoted in *Under the Influence* p19
"six to eight vedros of vodka": Patricia. Herlihy, "Joy of the Rus" Rites and Rituals of Russian Drinking" in *Russian Review*, Vol. 50, No. 2 (April 1991) pp131–147
"everyone had already regaled themselves well…": quoted in Stephen White, *Russia goes Dry* p8
"the epitome of pleasure…": quoted in Patricia Herlihy, *The Alcoholic Nation* p 71
"You didn"t pay respects to me…": quoted in *Under the Influence* p20
"Vodka is served immediately…": Olga Semyonova Tian-Shanskaia, *Village Life in Late Tsarist Russia* p16
"the secular soul of rural Russia…" Alan Kimball, *The Village Kabak as an Expression of Russian Civil Society, 1855–1905* as unpaginated document: http://pages.uoregon.edu/kimball/kbk.htm
"always on the look-out for drunkards" and subsequent quotations:

W.R.S. Ralston, *Good Words* p635
Painting by Leonid Ivanovich Solomatkin: *Morning at the Tavern,* State Art Museum, Irkutsk, Siberia, Russia
Painting by Vasily Grigorievich Perov: *The Last Tavern at the City Gates*, The Tretyakov Gallery, Moscow Russia
"thinner than water…"; "O to be drunk!..." and "...scalds the tongue but leaves you sober…" Иван Гаврилович Прыжов, *История кабаков в России в связи с историей русского народа* [Ivan Gavrilovic Pryzhov, *History of taverns in Russia]* p230
The Official birth of Vodka
"this slush is poured into bottles…": Himelstein, p149
"not by the amount of income derived by the State…": Sergei Witte, *The Memoirs of Count Witte*, p56
"The Russian Minister of Finance has presented…": in *Anglo-Russian News, London* May 1897
"the Japanese found several thousand Russian soldiers…": George E. Snow in Jahrbücher für Geschichte Osteuropas [Germany] 1997 45(3) p427
"The vodka casks were hacked open with knives…": Francis McCullagh *With the Cossacks* p248
"distorted the meaning of the reform…": Witte, *Memoirs* p55
"habitual consumers but not so high…": Witte, *Memoirs* p57
"men and women, adults and mere youngsters…": Witte, *Memoirs* p371
"was saved by the would be assassins…": in *The Guardian* August 27, 1906
"a man of no mind or no will…": in *The Observer*, Sep 2, 1906
"drinkers who previously remained hidden…": Joan Neuberger, *Hooliganism crime, culture and power in St. Petersburg, 1900-1914* p31
"the so-called 'Hooliganism'…": Herlihy, *The Alcoholic nation* p137
" 'tragic scenes of the degeneration of the people'…" quoted in Himelstein, *The King of Vodka* p273
"and 20,000 arrests were made in one day…": in *The Guardian* April

25, 1914
"highly improbable that they could accept… it must not be forgotten that the Russian drink-shops…": *The Guardian* April 25, 1914
"He was impressed with my recital…": *New York Times*, November 19, 1914
"the tsar's firm will to abolish…": and subsequent quotations: *The Guardian*, Nov 20 1914
"and were as 'merry as funerals'…": Stephen Frank & Mark D. Steinberg (eds.) *Cultures in flux* p 97
"categorically that the Government will encourage temperance…": *The Guardian* January 4, 1916
"Rasputin came out…": www.alexanderpalace.org/palace/rasputin-report.html
"It is perfectly plain that if you interfere…": Commander Hon. Joseph Kenworthy, *Hansard* November 5, 1919

Soviet Russia

"Stalin belatedly discovered the virtues of vodka…" Nicholas Ermochkine & Peter Ilikowski, *Forty Degrees East* p64
"no trade in rotgut…": Transchel, *Under the Influence:*, p149
"…I told him about an occasion…": Richard Taylor & D. W. Spring, *Stalinism and Soviet Cinema* p23
"What is better, the yoke of foreign capital…": Transchel, *Under the Influence* p149
"mixing Georgian wine, brandy and vodka…": Nicholas Ermochkine & Peter Ilikowski, *Forty Degrees East* p7
"Everyone drank…": Herlihy, *The Alcoholic Nation,* p52
Story of stamp clerk in *The Times* April 17 1928
"We demand sober parents…": *Russia goes Dry* p25
"…Where can we find the money?…": *Stalin's Letters to Molotov 1925–1936* p 209
The propaganda film *The General Line* in *The Times* September 24,

1929
"We'll find a bullet...": http//englishrussia.com/2009/07/09/some-facts-about-vodka-in-the-ussr/
"Why are you looking at me like that?...": Nicholas Ermochkine & Peter Ilikowski, *Forty Degrees East* p 64
"...was in a state of collapse": Budu Svanidzé, *My Uncle, Joseph Stalin* p217
"...vodka flowed freely and one's glass kept being filled up..." and subsequent quotations: FM Lord Alanbrooke: *War Diaries 1939–1945* – pp302–303
"impervious to any quantity of alcohol": Tim Tzouliadis, *The Forsaken* p66
"I wish they had given us two hundred grams of vodka" and "Let's drink to Stalin...": (ed) Vladimir A. Kozlov, *Sedition* p74
"...I tried to spill some of the drink over my shoulder..." Leo Kolber with L. Ian MacDonald, *Leo a life* p 143
"the biggest state in the world..." and subsequent quotations "Duke, Merry Christmas, Nikita": Michael Munn, *John Wayne* pp204–206
"the reasons for drinking have been eliminated..." *The Guardian* Aug 8 1964
The story of factory visit by Brezhnev http//www.bellybuttonwindow.com/1998/russia/i_love_me_some_vodka.html
"The Russians have always drunk vodka..." Andrei Gromyko, *Houston Chronicle* April 4, 1989
"One of the drinkers is a lady!..." White, *Russia goes Dry* p271
"where original sin... does not burden anyone there..." Benedict Erofeev, *Moscow Circles* p 43
"White Lilac-50 grams... Lily of the Valley simply won't do..." Ibid. pp70, 71
Vodka in Poland and Ukraine
"Of the Poles – Miserable condition..." Edmund Spencer, *Travels in the western Caucasus,* Chapter heading
"could not but admire the fine manly forms..." *Travels in the western Caucasus,* p270
"the only vodka of comparable quality is produced by Pierre Smirnoff

of Russia": http//faino.home.pl/baczewski/index_gb.swf
"The Nazi occupation forces had deliberately fostered Poland…" in *The Guardian* Dec 11, 1958
"keep an otherwise discontented people happy…" *Forty Degrees East* p 9
"stinks of the W.C…" Bartlett, *Scenes from a life,* p113
"The people at the bottling plant just wanted to use…" *Drinks International*, March 2011 p22
"I think it's important that this is viewed as the small man…" *Drinks International,* March 2011 p23
"We're getting a great response to the history…" *Drinks International,* March 2011 p18

Smirnoff to Absolut: The Vodka Houses

Himelstein *The King of Vodka* 328
"There is a new drink that is a craze…" E[d]ith Gynn, *The Hollywood Reporter*, 27 December 1942 cited in http//www.webtender.com/iforum/message.cgi?id=69904
"Smirnoff go home…" Wayne Curtin, *And a bottle of rum* p211
Campaign supplement European brands; Born again brands December 1, 1995,
Campaign, Successful with Advertising for Smirnoff Vodka, March 14, 1997 p41.
"With this redesign, we are looking to encapsulate" http//www.finecut.co.uk/blog/2010/7/smirnoff-reveals-new-packaging
Most of the information about the Absolut bottle design is from Carl Hamilton, *Absolut*
"One visual message is that opening…" Jonathan E. Schroeder, *Visual Consumption* p157
"free-spending, brand-fickle consumers ages 21 to 29…" Media/Advertising *The New York Times,* September 3, 2004
"challenges the *status quo* by presenting…" http//www.prnewswire.com/news-releases/absolutr-launches-global-advertising-

campaign-58826012.html April 27 2007
"In no way was it meant to offend or disparage..." in *Time Magazine*, April 8 2008, http//www.time.com/time/world/article/0,8599,1728801,00.html#ixzz1ouKx5ibO
"endorsing alcohol, tobacco and guns..." http//adage.com/article/briefs/week/99497/ June 7, 2004

Vodka in the UK and the USA

"began to market a British vodka..." in *The Times,* April 27, 1954
"first to introduce..." in *The Times* 30 Apr. 1958
"HERE'S PROOF 140%..." in *Illustrated London News* April 27, 1957
"wondrously, breathlessly smooth..." in *Crossbow* vols 3–4 1959 p58
"at some cost to his health and pocket..." and "increasing fairly fast and fairly substantially..." *Hansard, vol 228 cc275-348, House of Lords Deb* 2 February 1961
"you could drink vodka without becoming fat..." and "...obviously likely to be the sort of drink..." Ibid.
"...a rough, fiery spirit likely to lead the drinker into unspeakable excesses..." and "contrary to popular belief..." in *The Times* Oct 10, 1962
"George Jessel"s newest pick-me-up..." *New York Herald Tribune* December 2, 1939
Advertisement in *Life* – 19 Sep 1955, p101
Bloody Mary Dennis Wheatley, *The Eight Ages of Justerini's 1749–1965* pp95–6
Cocktail recipes selected from: G. Selmer Fougner, *Along The Wine Trail*

James Bond and Films

"its filtration through activated charcoal is a help..." Ian Fleming,

Goldfinger, p172
"Shaken, not stirred sir?..." Looney Tunes *Back* in *Action* (2003)
The details of the laboratory report on Bond are found at http//www.ncbi.nlm.nih.gov/pmc/articles/PMC28303/
"First tasted the vodkas... *"New Scientist,* June 5–11, 2010
"mutually beneficial practice by which companies pay..." *Los Angeles Magazine*, May, 1998 p30 "Shaken, Not Stirred, But No Longer..." Christopher Lawton, in *Wall Street Journal*, September 18, 2002 "more in the 21–29 age group..." Ibid.
From The Simpsons *When You Dish Upon a Star* (1989)
"The great thing is that because..." *The Daily Telegraph,* 21 Apr 2011

Vodka Today

"St. Petersburg, which follows trends established in Moscow..." *Drinks International* Vodka Supplement 2011 p 23
"crafting truly artisanal spirits of uncompromising quality..." http//www.sipsmith.com/
"tired of the message dripping off vodka packaging..." *The Independent*, August 18, 2010
"people will move away from consuming vodka..." Ibid.
"The story and quality are obviously key these days" Alex Kammerling in *Drinks International* Vodka Supplement_2011 p23
"tired of the message dripping off vodka packaging..." and "people will move away..." *The Independent*, August 18, 2010
"The story and quality are obviously key..." *Drinks International* Vodka Supplement 2011 p23
"neutral spirits so distilled..." http//www.access.gpo.gov/nara/cfr/waisidx_03/27cfr5_03.html discerning drinker."

Russian Writers: Tolstoy, Dostoevsky, Pryzhov and Chekhov

"I fornicated and practised deceit...": Leo Tolstoy, *A Confession* p 22
"I remember being struck by the evidence of a cook...": Leo Tolstoy, *The Complete Works, Volume 23* p557
"the evils of alcohol, strongly urging them not to touch it...": Sofia Tolstoy, *Diaries of Sofia Tolstoy* p171
"a well-spread supper table awaited us...": Aylmer Maude, *The Life of Tolstoy Later years* p373
"showed how much he sympathised...": Maude, *The Life of Tolstoy* p340
"quite clear that only those were guilty..." http//www.liquorpress.com/2011/04/15/vodka-and-russian-literature/
"favour of removing the Imperial Eagle...": *The Guardian* June 1, 1908
"Directly across the street from the inn": Fyodor Dostoevsky, *A Writer's Diary* pp327–330
"his whole life had been a dog's life...": Abbott Gleason, *Russian Revolutionaries* p367
"one of the most important events...": in *Dostoevsky Studies*, Volumes 2–6, 1981 p27
"Tolkachenko – a strange individual, a man who was already about forty...": Fyodor Dostoyevsky *Demons* p433
"The Russian God has already given up..." and "seas and oceans of vodka..." *Demons* pp510, 408
"stop any passer-by and ask..." Joseph Bradley, *Muzhik and Musocovite* p254
"who was willing to sell his manuscripts...": Yury Trifonov, *The Long Goodbye* pp243, 255
"Who keeps the tavern...": Anton Chekhov, *The Russian Master and Other Stories* p170
"[Chekhov] was very hospitable and loved it..." Alexander Kuprin, *Reminiscences of Anton Chekhov* p30 "Taught... to drink beer..." Chekhov, *The Russian Master and Other Stories* p36 "The Russian

is a great pig…" Anton Chekhov, *Letters of Anton Chekhov to His Family and Friends* p197
"vowed to establish temperance in this district…" Chekhov, *The Marshal's Widow* p141

Vodka and Music

"…the more sensitive, more responsive writers…" Solomon Volkov, *St. Petersburg: A Cultural History* p87
"…An intense worship of Bacchus…" Volkov, *St. Petersburg: A Cultural History* p87
"Talented people in Russia…" Volkov, *St. Petersburg: A Cultural History* p87
"…everything good in…" Volkov, St. *Petersburg: A Cultural History* p87
"Mme. Cécile Chaminade might safely…" Sergei Bertensson, *Sergei Rachmaninoff* p250
"On the dirty table…" Matthew Boyden & Nick Kimberley, *The Rough Guide to the Opera*, p334
"It is said that to abuse oneself…" P.I. Tchaikovsky, *The Diaries of Tchaikovsky* p246
"fierce whiskers stained with vodka" Nicolas Slonimsky, *Writings on Music*, p33
"Russian vodka with French perfumes…" Igor Stravinsky & Robert Craft, *Memories and Commentaries* p55
"the soldier tricks the Devil…" Igor Stravinsky & Robert Craft, *Expositions and developments* p90
"…with a great big glass…" Ira Gitler, *Swing to Bop* p194

How Smirnov became Smirnoff: A History of a Dynasty

"In 1886 Pierre Smirnoff produced…": Advertisement in the *New Yorker*, September 27, 1982
"afflicted by the tape worm…": *The Annals of philosophy, Volume*

3 p162
"by merely shaking corn-based spirit…": *Cuba: The Legend of Rum* p54
"the most remarkable vodka there is…": Linda Himelstein, *The King of Vodka* p76, "Smirnov started to accept numerous calls…": Himelstein p76 "cannot be complied with since…": Himelstein p65 "For many years, I have been trading…": Himelstein p129 "for the table wine, vodka, liqueurs and for grape wine too": Himelstein p136 "All the stores of grape wine, cognac, flavoured vodka…": Himelstein p291
" '*No 21*' did not resemble the Moscow vodka…": В. П. Смирнов, *Русский характер* [V.P. Smirnov, *Smirnov a Russian character*] p76

Wine and vodka list of Ivan Smirnov

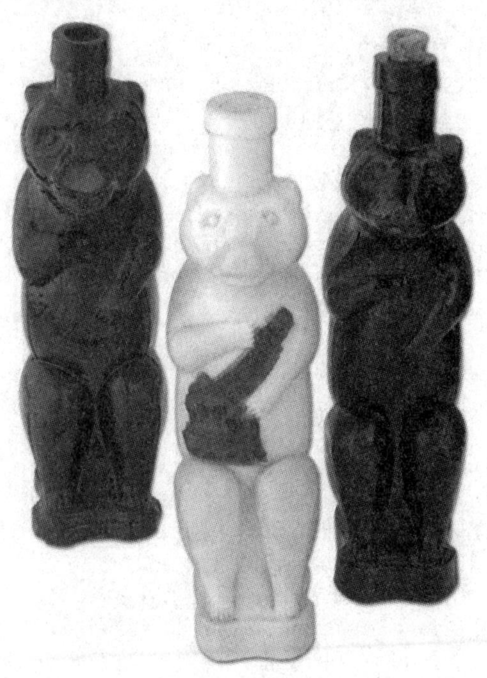

Smirnov Bears vodka bottles

Bibliography

Abbott, Gleason *Young Russia: The Genesis of Russian Radicalism in the 1860s* (Viking Press, 1980)

Alanbrooke, Viscount (Alex Danchev & Daniel Todman, eds) *War Diaries 1939-1945* (Weidenfeld & Nicolson, 2001)

Amis, Kingsley *Everyday Drinking* (Bloomsbury, 2009)

An Observer *Message from Moscow* (Cape, 1964)

Baker, Phil *The Dedalus Book of Absinthe* (Dedalus Books, 2001)

Barnett, Richard *The Dedalus Book of Gin* (Dedalus Books, 2011)

Barr, Andrew *Drink* (Bantam Press, 1995)

Bartlett, Rosamund *Chekhov: Scenes from a Life* (Free Press, 2004)

Baur, Duane A. *Vodka and Russia* (TCC Humanities, Saint Petersburg n.d.)

Berry, Lloyd E. & Crummey, Robert O., (eds) *Rude and Barbarous Kingdom* (University of Wisconsin Press, 1968)

Blundy, Anna *Neat Vodka* (Sphere, 2007)

Boyden, Matthew & Kimberley, Nick *The Rough Guide to the Opera* (Rough Guides, 2002)

Bradley, Joseph *Muzhik and Muscovite* (University of California Press, 1985)

Brown, Jared McDaniel, Miller, Anistatia Renard & Broom, Dave *Cuba: The Legend of Rum* (Mixellany Limited, 2009)

Browne, John Ross *The Land Of Thor* (Harper & Brothers,1867)

Bulgakov, Mikhail *The Master & Margarita* (Picador, 1995)

Chekhov, Anton *The Russian master and other stories* (O.U.P.,1999)

Chekhov, Anton (Avrahm Yarmolinsky, ed) *Letters* (Cape, 1974)

Cross, Anthony *By the Banks of the Neva* (C.U.P, 1997)

Curtin, Wayne *And a bottle of rum* (Crown Press,1996)

De Witte, Sergei *The Memoirs of Count de Witte,* (Doubleday, 1921)

Dickens, Geoffrey *The Courts of Europe* (Greenwich House,1984)

Dostoevsky, Fyodor *Devils* (Wordsworth Editions 2005)

Dostoevsky, Fyodor *Notes from a Dead House* (Wordsworth Editions 2010)

Dostoevsky, Fyodor (trs Kenneth Lanz) *Writer's Diary* (Northwestern University Press 2009)

Dunkling, Leslie *The Guinness Drinking Companion* (Guinness Publishing, 1992

Emerson, Edward R *Beverages, Past and Present Vol 1* (G. P. Putnam, 1908)

Ermochkine, Nicholas & Iglikowski, Peter *Forty Degrees East: an anatomy of vodka* (Nova Publishers, 2004)

Erofeev, Benedict (J.R. Dorrell, trs.) *Moscow Circles* (Writers and Readers Publishing Co-operative, 1981)

Feifer, George *Justice in Moscow* (Simon & Schuster, 1964)

Figes, Orlando *A People's Tragedy* (Cape, 1996)

Fleming, Ian *Thunderball* (Signet Classics, 1953)

Fleming, Ian *Goldfinger* (Penguin Books, 2006)

Fougner, G. Selmer *Along The Wine Trail, An Anthology of Wines and Spirits* (The Sun Printing & Publishing Assoc., 1934)

Frank, Stephen, P. & Steinberg, Mark D. (eds) *Cultures in Flux* (Princeton University Press,1994)

Geldern, James von & McReynolds, Louise (eds) *Entertaining Tsarist Russia* (Indiana University Press, 1998)

Georgi, J.G. (W. Took, trs.) *Russia: or, a compleat historical account Vol ii,* (T. Cadell, 1780)

Gerould, Daniel (ed) *The Witkiewicz Reader* (Northwestern University Press, 1992)

Gogol, Nikolai (Richard Pevear & Larissa Volokhonsky, trs.) *The Collected Tales* (Granta Books, 1998)

Gelasimov, Andrei (Marian Schwartz, trs.) Thirst (Amazon

Crossing, 2011)

Gitler, Ira *Swing to Bop: An Oral History of the Transition in Jazz in the 1940s* (O.U.P 1985)

Goodrich, Joseph King *Russia in Europe and Asia* (A.C. McClurg & Co. 1912)

Gordin, A. *Pushkin's St. Petersburg* (Khudonik, 1991)

Gordin, Michael *Dimitri Mendeleev and the shadow of the Periodic Table* (Basic Books, 2004)

Hamilton, Carl *Absolut* (Texere, 2000)

Helenius, Karl *The Russian Charka. The Silver Vodka Cup of the Romanov Era 1613–1917* (Helsinki 2006)

Henningsen, Charles Frederick *The white slave: or, The Russian peasant girl: Vol. 3* (Henry Colburn, 1845)

Herlihy, Patricia *The Alcoholic Empire* (O.U.P, 2002)

Himelstein, Linda *The King of Vodka: The Story of Pyotr Smirnov* (Harper Collins, 2009)

Kelly, Laurence (ed) *Moscow* (Robinson, 2004)

Kelly, Laurence (ed) *St. Petersburg* (Robinson, 2003)

Kimball, Alan *The Village Kabak as an Expression of Russian Civil Society, 1855-1905* (Russian Academy of Sciences, 2002)

King, Greg & Wilson, Penny *The Fate of the Romanovs* (Wiley, 2003)

Kohl, J.G. *Russia and the Russians in 1842* (Carey & Hart, 1842)

Kozlov, Vladimir A. & Mironenko, Sergei V. (eds.) *Sedition: Everyday Resistance in the Soviet Union Under Khrushchev and Brezhnev* (Yale, 2011)

Lyall, Robert *The Character Of The Russians And A Detailed History Of Moscow* (Blackwood, 1823)

Marsden, Christopher *Palmyra of the North* (Faber, 1942)

Massie, Robert K. *Peter the Great* (Ballantine Books, 1980)

Merridale, Catherine *Night of Stone* (Granta Books, 2000

Mitchell, T *Handbook for Travellers in Russia, Poland and Finland* (Murray, 1865)

Montefiore, Simon Sebag *Stalin: the Court of the Red Tsar* (Phoenix, 2004)

Morris, R.M. *The Cleansing Flames* (Faber, 2011)

Munn, Michael *John Wayne: The Man Behind the Myth* (Robson, 2004)

Neuberger, Joan *Hooliganism* (University of California Press, 1993

Olearius, Adam (Samuel H. Baron, ed) *The Travels of Olearius in Seventeenth-Century Russia* (Stanford University Press, 1967)

Ometev, Boris & Stuart, John *St. Petersburg* (Vendome Press, 1990)

Oswald, Felix L. *Popular Science Monthly Volume 33 May* (New York 1888)

Pitcher, Harvey *Muir and Mirrielees* (Swallow House Books, 1994)

Pitcher, Harvey *When Miss Emmie was in Russia* (John Murray, 1977)

Poznansky, Alexander *Tchaikovsky: The Quest for the Inner Man* (Schirmer Books, 1991)

Pokhlebkin, William (Renfrey Clarke, trs.) *A History of Vodka* (Verso, 1992)

Radzinsky, Edvard *The Rasputin File* (Doubleday, 2000)

Ralston, W.R.S *Good Words for October 1st 1868* ed *Norman MacLeod* (Strahan & Co., 1868)

Riasanovsky, Nicholas *The Image of Peter the Great in Russian History and Thought* (O.U.P., 1992)

Ritchie, Leitch *Russia and the Russians* (Cary and Hart, 1836)

Ryan, William *The Bloody Meadow* (Mantle, 2011)

Sala, George Augustus *A Journey Due North in the Summer of 1856* (Richard Bentley, 1858)

Segal, Boris M *The Drunken Society – Alcohol Abuse and Alcoholism in the Soviet Union* (Hippocrene Books, 1990)

Volkov, Solomon *St. Petersburg: A Cultural History* (New York, 1995)

Sellers, Robert *An A-Z of Hellraisers* (Arrow, 2011)

Smith, Robert E. F. & Christian, David *Bread and salt* (C.U.P., 1984)

Stravinsky, Igor & Craft, Robert *Expositions and developments* (University of California Press, 1981)

Stravinsky, Igor & Craft, Robert *Memories and Commentaries* (University of California Press, 1981)

Tatlock, Lynne (ed) *Seventeenth century German prose* (Continuum Publication Company, 2003)

Tatyana, Tolstaya, *Pushkin's Children* (Houghton & Mifflin, NY, 2003)

Taylor, Richard & Spring, D.W *Stalinism and Soviet cinema* (Routledge, 1993)

Tchaikovsky, Peter I, (ed) Wlaidmir Lakond *Diaries of Tchaikovsky* (W.W. Norton, 1945)

Thomas Thomson, Richard Phillips, Edward William Brayley (eds) *The Annals of philosophy, Vol. 3* (Baldwin Craddock & Joy, 1814)

Tian-Shanskaia, Olga Semyonova (David L. Ransel ed, Michael Levine, trs.) *Village Life in Late Tsarist Russia,* (Indiana University Press, 1993)

Tolstoy, Leo *The complete works of Count Tolstoy, Volume 23* (J. M. Dent & Co., 1905)

Tolstoy, Leo (Jane Kentish, ed) *A Confession And Other Religious Writings,* (Penguin, 1987)

Tolstoy, Sofia (trs. Cathy Porter) *The Diaries of Sofia Tolstoy* (Alma Books, 2010)

Transchel, Kate *Under the Influence* (University of Pittsburgh Press, 2006)

Turberville, George *Letters* in *Richard Hakluyt, The Principall Navigations, Volume 4* (Kessinger Publishing, 2004)

Tzouliadis, Tim *The Forsaken* (Abacus, 2008)

Vitaliev, Vitali *Borders Up! Eastern Europe through the bottom of a Glass* (Scribner, 1999)

Voyce, Arthur *Moscow* (David & Charles, 1972)

Warnes, David *Chronicle of the Russian Tsars* (Thames & Hudson, 1994)

Wheatley, Dennis *The Eight Ages of Justerini's 1749-1965*

(Dolphin Publishing, n.d. [1965])

White, Stephen *Russia goes Dry* (C.U.P., 1996)

Wisniewski, Ian *Vodka* (Ryland Peters & Small, 2003)

Wood, Henry *My Life of Music* (Ayer Publishing, 1946)

Books in Russian

Александр В. Никишин & К. В Смирнова, (редакторы) *Владимире Петровиче Смирнов Русский Характер* (Вагриус , 2004)

[Alyeksandr V. Nikishin & K. V Smirnova Vladimirye Pyetrovichye Smirnov Roosskiy Xaraktyer

Vladimir Peter Smirnov: A Russian Character]

Государственный музей истории Санкт-Петербурга *Вино и водка в Петербурге* (Санкт-Петербурга, 2006)

[Vino i vodka v Peterburg

Wine and vodka of Petersburg]

Есипов В.В, *Житие великого грешника: Документально-лирическое повествование о судьбе русского пьяницы и замечательного историка-самоучки Ивана Гавриловича Прыжова* (Русская панорама, 2011)

[Zhitiye vyelikogo gryeshnika: Dokoomyental'no-lirichyeskoye vyestvovaniye o sood'bye roosskogo p'yanitsi i zamyechatyel'nogo istorika-samooochki Ivana Gavrilovicha Prizhova

Yesipov V.V. *Life of a Great Sinner: Documentary lyrical story about the fate of a Russian drunkard and a remarkable self-taught historian Ivan Gavrilovic Pryzhova*]

Курукин, Игорь & Никулина, *Елена Повседневная жизнь русского кабака от Ивана Грозного до Бориса Ельцина* (Молодая гвардия, 2007)

[Koorookin, Igor' & Nikoolina, Yelyena

Povsyednyevnaya zhizn' roosskogo kabaka ot Ivana Groznogo

do Borisa Yel'tsina

Everyday life of a Russian tavern from Ivan the Terrible to Boris Yeltsin]

Кручинин, Евгений, *Водка* (Eksmo /BBPG, 2009)

[Kruchina, Evgenij. *Vodka]*

Кричевский, Виталий *русская водка: Письма моему швейцарскому другу* (Деан, 2002)

[Krichyevskiy, Vitaliy Russian vodka: Pis'ma moyemoo shvyeytsarskomoo droogoo]

Russian Vodka: Letters to my Swiss Friend]

Никишин А. В. *водка и сталин (*Дом Русской Водки, 2006)

[Nikishin, A.V. Vodka i Stalin

Vodka and Stalin]

Овсянников, Юрий Khudozhnik *Лубок*(Советский, 1968

[Ovsiannikov, Yurii *Lubok*

Похлёбкин, Вильям Васильевич *Ро История водки* (Центрполиграф, 2005

(History of vodka)

Прыжов, Иван Гаврилович История Кабаковв России В Связи С Историей Русского Народа (Авалонъ, 2009)

[Pryzhov, Ivan Gabrovolich *Istoriia Kahakov V Rossii V Sviazi S Istoriei Russkago*

History Of Taverns In Russia In Connection With The History Of The Russian People]

Шумейко И.Н 10 мифов о русской водке (Eksmo, 2009)

[Šumejko, I. N

10 Mifov O Russkoj Vodke

Ten Myths about Russian Vodka]

Acknowledgements

The standard work on vodka, *A History of Vodka* by William Pokhlebkin, was first published in Russia in 1991 but was unfortunately shortened when it appeared in a fine translation in the UK in 1992. The author was murdered in his home near Moscow in 2000, and his body was discovered by his publisher, the grandson of Boris Pasternak. The murder remains unsolved. Although biased towards Russian vodka, Pokhlebkin produced a fine, provocative and scholarly book.

40 Degrees East: An Anatomy of Vodka by Nicholas Ermochkine and Peter Iglikowski, writers of Russian and Polish descent respectively, is a balanced and an amusing account of the spirit. I am particularly grateful to the writers of these two books.

I have to thank the many friends who helped in the preparation of this book, not least those who were persuaded to taste many different vodkas and comment on them.

Mark Watson endured a freezing trudge through the Moscow snow and ice. Without his expert navigation of the Moscow Underground, I would probably still be stranded there. Dermot Wilson joined us in St. Petersburg and selected excellent vodkas in some of the city's taverns.

For help in finding books, I owe a debt of gratitude to Richard Bull and Andrew Kruszelnicki. William Ryan kindly paused his work on the exploits of his fictional Moscow detective Korolev to give me information on sources, and I am grateful for his suggestions.

Jen Gordon of Diageo very helpfully contacted the Smirnoff archivist who located useful information about the Smirnoff label and thus solved a mystery for me. I am grateful to Ekaterina Mikhailovna Kulishova of the Moscow Vodka Museum and her colleagues for their courtesy and help during my visit. I am also in the debt of Irina Karpenko of the State Museum of the History of St Petersburg, who kindly sent me free of charge an otherwise unobtainable book. Patricia Herlihy and Linda Himelstein, who have made their own valuable contributions to the study of vodka, kindly answered my questions. The author of a study on the Russian *charka,* Karl Helenius of Helsinki, identified some objects for me. Jacob Khokhlov was extremely helpful over a problematical Russian translation, while Stephen Oakes kindly gifted Soviet temperance matchbox labels.

Kyri Sotiri of Soho Wine Supply shared his wide knowledge of vodka and showed me his large stock from all parts of the world. David Youl contributed his expert knowledge of cocktails, while his family cooked delicious meals for us.

Tiko Tuskadze of Little Georgia Restaurants generously shared her knowledge of vodka and I am grateful for her advice.

Riri Girardon and Malcom Barker of The Studio Barker-Girardon photographed vodka cups and the *zakuski*. For this and many other kindnesses, I am extremely indebted.

Jocelyn Burton, with the assistance of Peter Lunn and Hal Messel produced a new vodka cup for this book. The photograph and the design of the cup are her copyright.

My predecessors in this Dedalus series, Phil Baker and Richard Barnett, wrote books on absinthe and gin respectively which have provided daunting but encouraging standards of excellence. I thank them both and Anthony Lane and the team at Dedalus.

I would like to say thank you to others who have helped me in diverse ways: Eugene Ankeny, Clive and Diana Barrett, Clive Boutle of Francis Boutle Publishers, Steve Broadhurst, Sheena Cameron, Alan Carr, Bill Carrick, Derek Collen, Dan Edelstyn, Gillian Elborn, Dave Ellis, Nick Hare, Ann Hawker, Ged and Maggie Holmyard, Frank and Barbara Joynt, Diana Leslie, Paul and Anne Marie Luscombe, Su McArthur, Bruna Mazzucchi, Craig Mollinson, Georgiana de Montfort, Jean Moore, Maureen Moore, Victoria Moore, Tim Oates, Chris R. Parker, Anne and Terry Parnaby, Jane Poncia, Sandy Robertson, Carole Samson, Paul Sharp, Jane Spiers,

Tommy Thompson, Christine Ward, Maryann Wilkins and Derin Young. Finally, it would be remiss of me not to thank a Moscow pigeon fancier who gave me some Russian verse but, alas, not his name.

The extract from *Angel Pavement* is reprinted by permission of United Agents on behalf of: The Estate of J. B. Priestley, and the extract from *Goldfinger* by Ian Fleming is reproduced with the permission of Ian Fleming Publications Ltd, London, www.ianfleming.com, and is copyright © of Ian Fleming Publications Ltd 1959.

The extract from *A Writer's Diary*, by F. Dostoevsky, reprinted by permission of Northwestern University Press. (*A Writer's Diary copyright* © 2009 by Northwestern University Press, Published 2009. All rights reserved.)

The images on pages 92, 103 and 109 have been reproduced courtesy of Diageo plc, owners of the SMIRNOFF® brand.

Maltsov glass vodka set

Ivan Smirnov vodka label

Index